WAKE UP CALL

What Every Young Adult Must Know To Survive Today's Job Market

Jeff Gunhus

This book may be purchased for educational, business or sales promotional use. For information, please write Special Promotions, 1683 Langley, Irvine, CA 92614 or visit www.thecareerseries.com

Printed in the United States of America

Library of Congress Cataloging-in-Publication Data

Gunhus, Jeff

Wake Up Call - What Every Young Adult Must Know To Survive Today's Job Market / Jeff Gunhus

ISBN-13: 978-1-4486-5507-6
ISBN-10: 1-4486-5507-2

For Nicole, Jack, William, Daniel and Caroline

I would like to thank the thousands of college students who have completed the College Works Painting internship program.

Your work ethic, perseverance and determination have been my constant source of inspiration.

For the thousands of participants yet to come...you have a tough act to follow.

TABLE OF CONTENTS

Author's Note

Parts of this book's content first appeared in <u>No Parachute</u> <u>Required – Translating Your Passion Into A Paycheck – And A</u> <u>Career </u>(Hyperion -2001). <u>No Parachute Required</u> was my first book and it was a thrilling experience to have it published.

There were some great moments.

Getting the call from my agent that the book had sold.

Receiving the first copy by mail.

Coming off the plane in Chicago with my wife and walking past an airport bookstore with a pyramid display built with dozens of my books.

Good stuff.

The hard part of the experience came quickly after as I began to notice all the things I wanted to change about the book.

I realized I had tried to do too much and the short how-to book I had imagined had somehow become 400 pages of dense text.

The whole point I wanted to make (do something audacious to separate yourself from your peers and then use Top Down Job Hunting to get the career offer no-one else can get) was lost in a sea of self-discovery exercises, long analogies and information overload. (I offer as evidence the full page I spent evaluating CD-ROMS available for purchase to help research target companies!)

So when the book had run its course and the rights reverted back to me, I was intrigued.

Here was the opportunity to reorganize and rewrite the book the way I had originally imagined it.

And this time I would be pulling from a full eighteen years of experience working with college students and from the perspective as the co-CEO of a $40 million business.

It sounded like fun, but I hesitated.

Did the world really need another career book?

Finally, current events gave me the necessary push.

As I carefully studied the effect of the declining economy on college students about to enter the work force, I saw that the change in career prospects and the job hunt was going to be massive and long-lasting.

However, while this fact graced the front page of every newspaper and dominated the evening news, the hundreds of students I met were in complete denial about the impact the new economic reality was about to have on them.

As far as they were concerned, it was business as usual.

I met finance students who still hoped to become investment bankers for firms they didn't realize had ceased to exist the month before.

Others who thought they might go into "flipping houses", oblivious to the complete meltdown in the real estate market.

Still others who believed their newly minted college degrees were somehow going to protect them against unemployment.

College graduates can always get a jobs, right?

This complete disconnect from reality astounded me.

On a cross-country flight, I jotted down what I considered to be the wake up calls these college students needed to hear if they had any hope of success in this tough market.

I knew no amount of career advice would make a difference unless the young men and women using the advice first understood that the basic rules of the game had changed.

Not only that, but I felt they needed to hear these things right away before they ended up as more unemployment statistics.

WAKE UP CALL – What Every Young Adult Must Know To Survive Today's Job Market is my attempt to give college students the edge they need to not only survive the down economy, but to succeed in spite of it.

The good news is that in even the worse economy there will still be success stories.

It is my hope that this book serves as a wake up call to those individuals with the work ethic, tenacity and ambition to be one of them.

Good luck.

Jeff Gunhus

Introduction

Why should you listen to me?

Whenever I pick up a self-help type book, I immediately think to myself,

"Who the heck does this person think they are, telling me what to do?"

I pick the book up, flip it over to the author bio, and 9/10 times I put the book down still thinking,

"Who the heck does this person think they are, telling me what to do?"

Call me a skeptic, but I'm pretty certain that most self-help authors are pretty much full of crap.

Like those guys hawking their books on how to "Make a Million Dollars from your Living Room" who say they've made soooo much money that they wanted to share their secrets with others.

Right.

There is no quick fix.

Things that sound too good to be true are just that – too good to be true.

Always.

So, if you are like me and you are skeptical of advice from "experts" trying to sell you a book, let me give you a little background to put you at ease.

I'm not some grumpy old guy sitting in a human resources job complaining that young people these days just can't hack it.

I am in my 30s and the co-CEO of a $40 million organization with over 2000 employees.

The organization is composed primarily of two companies, Empire Community Painting and College Works Painting.

While Empire Community Painting is a leading commercial painting company in the Western U.S., my position in our student business, College Works Painting, is what has given me the experience to draw on to write this book.

College Works Painting teaches college students entrepreneurial and leadership skills by having them run a small house painting business for the summer.

The program is often cited as one of the top internships in the country and past participants have gone on to successful careers in business, finance, law, and medicine.

These alumni point to College Works Painting as the formative experience in their career development.

So, what does this have to do with you?

As a business-owner that hires over a 1200 students a year (from over 20,000 applicants), I have had a front-row seat in interviews with college students for the last eighteen years.

My organization has worked with literally tens of thousands of students on how to create marketable skills while in school and how to tackle the job market after graduation.

I have direct links to what is happening in the college hiring markets through relationships with career centers and major employers.

I know what works and what doesn't because I live it every day.

This is not some theory I'm testing.

Not some academic notion.

It's the unvarnished ground truth of how the job market is going to treat you once you graduate and how you can use this knowledge to your advantage.

I'm Not Here To Make Friends

Let's just get this out of the way.

You're not going to like a lot of things in this book, especially what I have to say in this first chapter.

In fact, you might even decide to not read this book because of it.

"Too negative."

"Condescending."

"Too in my face."

Fine.

Whatever.

But on these next few pages there are things you really need to know and understand if you're going to stand a chance in the real world.

You might choose to put this book down or you might be tempted to flip past the first chapter.

 That would be a mistake.

These are things you need to hear. Things you are not going to find in those feel-good, if-you-write-a-good-resume-they-will-come career guides that fill your college bookstore shelves.

And if you pay attention and really understand that these wake up calls apply to you, then we have a chance that you will actually use some of the techniques I'll teach you later in the book.

Techniques that will enable you to succeed while everyone around you is failing.

When most people get a wake up call, they just press the snooze button.

Others jump up and get busy chasing their goals and dreams.

What are you going to do?

The choice is yours.

Chapter One

WAKE UP CALLS

**12 Inconvenient Truths Every Young Adult
Needs To Hear**

WAKE UP CALL #1 - The world has changed. It's tough now and it's going to get worse.

Your timing could have been better.

Before you got here, times were pretty good.

First there was the technology boom where it seemed anyone with a day trading account and a dart board could make a quick fortune.

During that same time, fresh-faced college grads found themselves lured to start-up companies with stock options that often turned into big paydays, sometimes worth millions.

Traditional employers battled back and developed perks and comp plans and vacation policies to compete for Gen X and Gen Y talent.

Then real estate was the new thing. Everyone got "zero down" loans and flipped houses.

Money flowed.

Life was easy.

Then, in a blink of an eye, it was all gone.

Bummer, huh?

The world financial markets collapsed, real estate values plummeted and behemoths like GM declared bankruptcy.

Employers everywhere woke up and had the same resounding thought, "Workers need me more than I need them."

And, my dear job-seeker, that new ground truth for employers is not good news for you.

A few headlines:

COLLEGE GRADUATES TACKLE DISMAL JOB MARKET – CBS News

COLLEGE GRADS FACE TOUGHEST MARKET IN YEARS – ABC News

COLLEGE DEGREE NO SHIELD AS MORE JOBS ARE SLASHED – Washington Post

Some stats from the 2009 National Association Of Colleges and Employers (NACE) *Student Survey*.

- Jobless rate for college graduates DOUBLED with over 2 million college graduates unemployed.

- Employers will hire 22% fewer college graduates this year.

- Only 19.7% of graduating seniors who actively sought jobs in 2009 landed one before graduation.

- 40% of graduating seniors believe they will find a job but will still need financial help from their parents.

- CNN reports 80% of 2009 college graduates moved back in with their parents.

- As of July, 2009 the economy shed over 7,000,000 jobs!

And the really bad news?

The economy has gotten much worse since these surveys were taken!

And don't fool yourself that you can hide in grad school until this blows over (or that you can stretch out your undergrad a couple more years).

The changes happening in the economy are systemic and long-lasting.

Things will improve eventually, but even when they do, the job market will be tough for a long time and never return to the easy days of multiple job offers at firms eager to entice you with creative perks. Which leads me to my next point...

WAKE UP CALL #2 – The negative impact of graduating into a bad economy will last for the first 10-15 years of your career.

I have to admit, this one even surprised me.

I thought it reasonable to assume that once the economy got back on its feet, recent college grads who had taken low-paying jobs to get by after graduation would just slide back into great career trajectories and get back on track.

Unfortunately for you, this is not the case.

A recent study by Yale economist Lisa Kahn found that college students who graduate in recessions experience a significant decrease in compensation for the first 10+ years of their careers.

When will the good news end, right?

Ms. Kahn's research attempted to understand why the phenomenon occurred. While it's impossible to assign the entire effect to one cause, she does put forward a likely explanation.

Evidence shows that college grads that enter the job market in a recession are forced to take jobs of a lesser stature than college grads graduating in normal or good economic times.

New entrants into the job market slave away at these "make-do" jobs for a couple of years, waiting out the recession.

Once the economic good times get back in full swing, they apply for, and often get, better jobs.

However, the skills developed at the lower paid "make-do" jobs rarely transfer into a useful skill in the new position, so the job seeker has to basically start all over.

For example, say a finance major graduates in 2010. No one in the finance world is hiring (and if they are, they can hire one of the thousands of laid-off finance gurus with **significant prior experience**), so the finance major gets a job with AT&T as a store manager.

Two years (and hundreds of cell phone upgrades later), the financial markets are hopping again and there are job openings at the investment banking firm that was once the finance major's dream job.

First, our poor finance major might not even apply. Once in the job market for 6 months or more, individuals become sedentary and resistant to change. Ever wonder why you see people with "10 Year Anniversary" badges checking your groceries at the supermarket?

Second, our finance major is a little out of touch with her finance background. She hasn't exactly been practicing derivative pricing models or modeling bond market fluctuations on her lunch breaks. Even with her "work experience" she might be a less attractive candidate than someone about to graduate who just crammed for their final in Advanced Financial Market Strategies.

Third, if she does get hired, our finance major will be essentially starting from square one next to recent grads 2-3 years younger than she.

What is really disappointing is that the statistics show that even in cases where the job candidate gets into their career 2-3 years after graduation, it will still take over 10 years for that grad to "catch-up" to where they should have been.

Unfair, isn't it?

The real question is, what are you going to do about it?

Complaining about the state of the economy is like complaining about the weather...it ain't gonna change anything.

All of the data shows that the negative effects of graduating during a recession come from taking a less-than-ideal job after graduation.

The solution?

You and I need to make sure you are one of the few who get a great job after graduation.

Even in a terrible economy, there are success stories and there are great jobs to be had. To get one, you will need to not only execute a flawless job search, but take the steps to turn yourself into an irresistible candidate.

The Career Series books can show you how, you just need to put in the time and the hard work.

If you don't, it could take you 10-15 years to recover from the mistake.

And it won't be easy because...

WAKE UP CALL #3 - Employers are done kissing up to you.

This is the big change.

Much has been made during the last 10 years of all the great things employers are doing to attract talent to their doors.

All the open space, casual every day, ping pong tables in the break room, techie companies that embraced the idea that Gen Y was different.

Gen Y was special and needed special treatment to massage their egos, stroke their self-esteem, and really tap into their...specialness.

No more.

Now a typical recruiter for a great job has more candidates than she knows what to do with.

These candidates, **<u>often with significant prior experience</u>**, don't care about the ping pong table in the break room, the health club in the basement or any of that claptrap.

Your new competition used to do the exact job someplace else before they were laid off.

They have families and house payments and child care costs and they are hungry for a job.

The bad news for you is that they have **significant prior experience.**

So, here you come, four years of college under your belt and some great resume-building vacations with your parents you've racked up over the past few summers (and one internship where you were "exposed" to your industry of choice while you filed papers and made photo-copies) and you want to know what the company can offer you if you choose to work for them.

Ha!

The days of employers kissing up to you are gone, gone, gone.

You want to work in finance on Wall Street? Get in line with the thousands and thousands of laid off workers with **significant prior experience.**

This new reality doesn't mean you can't get a job.

It means that if you want anything other than the most basic job after college, you have to elevate your game.

The job market used to be like you were an NBA player jumping into a high school game. You were a star and everyone wanted you to be team captain.

Now it has flipped.

You're the high school player finding yourself suddenly playing against the Lakers.

Doesn't mean you're going to get schooled.

It just means you need to figure out how to play the game to their level...and fast.

You need <u>significant prior experience.</u>

(Did I mention that already?)

WAKE UP CALL #4 - Your career will define who you are.

I know, I know.

"Your job is what you do, not who you are."

"Life is about more than just work."

I can give you plenty of other clever ways to justify trading hours for a paycheck so you don't feel so bad about wasting away at some meaningless job.

But the truth of the matter is that you are going to spend an enormous amount of your adult life either at work or thinking about work.

Let's do the math:

Each week has 168 hours. The average person sleeps 8 hours a night. That is 56 hours a week, leaving a balance of 112 waking hours. Once you take out some of the daily routines of life (commuting, showers, brushing your teeth, laundry, etc.), you are left with approximately 98 hours.

A career professional works at least 45 hours a week, <u>approximately one-half of the time you are awake each week!</u>

If you still don't get it, check out the typical week you will be living for the next 25-40 years.

One week	168 hours
Average sleep per week (8 hours a night)	- 56 hours
Average commute to work per week	- 4 hours
Average time on routine	- 16 hours
Average work week for career professional	- <u>45 hours</u>
Free time left	**= 47 hours**

*A.C. Neilsen Co. reports the average American watched 28 hours of TV a week! That is 9 years of TV watching over a 65 year lifetime!

Now tell me how do you feel about that resume filled with retail experience you spent 15 minutes creating on your PC?

How about those entry level position interviews you lined up at the career center simply because they were the only jobs left over on the schedule?

This whole job search thing is a pretty big deal. Time to treat it like one.

Are you still thinking that your job will not significantly impact the type of person you become?

How can you possibly believe that the way you spend half of your waking moments will not make an enormous impact on every other part of your life?

Do you really think that if you end up in a dissatisfying, dead-end job that simply pays the bills, that you will have the fulfilled life you're imagining for yourself?

The world already has too many clock-watchers, people trading half their waking hours for a paycheck and the promise of a great weekend and two weeks vacation a year.

Don't turn yourself into one more.

Why is this important?

Because, after we get done waking you up a little, I'm going to give you fool-proof steps to make yourself marketable and explain how to tap into the hidden sources of great jobs.

The problem is that all the steps require you to work for your success.

Unless you really "get" WAKE UP CALLS #1, #2, #3 and #4, we might as well pack our bags and head home.

A quick recap:

WAKE UP CALL #1: The economy has made it harder for you. This is true for the next decade.

WAKE UP CALL #2: If you don't get a great job after graduation, it could hurt you for 10-15 years.

WAKE UP CALL #3: Employers are not going to kiss up to you. They have hundreds of applicants for jobs they used to have to recruit at your campus to fill. You have to raise your game if you want to compete.

WAKE UP CALL #4: You will spend half of your waking hours at work! Anything you spend half you time doing is going to mold and form the person you become. Doesn't it make sense to invest time at the beginning to make sure you get it right?

I mean, this is your *life* we're talking about. Hopefully, I've gotten your attention.

WAKE UP CALL #5 - You need to go college (if you are currently in college, read this in case you get dumb some day and think about dropping out).

No other factor is a better predictor of economic well-being than education.

Not race.

Not gender.

Education.

My favorite reasons not to go to college.

College is not for everyone. That's crap. It's for everyone who wants to get ahead in life, care for their family, and open their minds to the world. I'm all about following your passion, but get yourself to college and you might change your mind about your "calling" to dig ditches for a living.

Can't afford it. Too bad, figure it out. Work two jobs. Work three jobs. No one said it would be easy. This isn't some MTV reality show, you have to work for your success. You have to work for your opportunity.

Bill Gates didn't go to college. Yeah, guess what? You're not Bill Gates.

The "opportunity cost is too high." So, you have some sweet job opportunity waiting for you and going to college will really mess it up?

Maybe, maybe not.

Often, the sweet job opportunity looks really great in the eyes of an 18-22 year old, but your 30 year old self will look back on that decision and laugh (or cry) that you passed up college to work as a manager for Office Depot so you could afford the payments on your new car.

Put it this way.

If you don't you'll likely find yourself at some point wishing you had.

If you do, I doubt you'll ever find yourself thinking, "Man, I wish I didn't have this college degree hanging around my neck."

Go to college. End of story.

WAKE UP CALL #6 - A college degree doesn't do anything for you.

OK. OK.

I get it.

I just spent all that ink and paper convincing you to either go to or stay in college...even though it doesn't do anything for you.

Let me explain.

Back in the day, a college degree opened doors.

It was as if multiple job offers were stapled to your diploma and you just had to decide which was best for you.

Those days? Long gone.

1.523 million people graduated from college in 2009.

Want to guess how many jobs have been lost during the recession?

Over 7,000,000 jobs.

Hmmm.....

In 2009, there were over 2 million unemployed college graduates.

This doesn't even begin to measure the chronically "under-employed" graduates.

You know the ones.

They are the people folding that shirt at the GAP you decided you didn't want.

Obviously, new college graduates are still getting jobs as they replace other workers in the economy. For example, low tech jobs are replaced by high tech jobs that require more training.

However, the simple fact is that there are literally hundreds of thousands more people with college degrees than there are jobs to go around.

I'm not even talking about life-changing, soul-inspiring, perfect-match-with-your-heart careers.

I'm just talking about jobs.

A college diploma is not enough.

Not nearly enough.

If you want to survive, you have to arm yourself with an amazing resume and with skills like never before.

You especially need **significant prior experience** if you want to be competitive.

So, since this is the new ground truth, do you really want to be in that candidate pool without a college degree as part of your arsenal?

Do you want to be the person with a diploma in one hand and a resume with fast food and retail experience in the other?

I don't think you do because it will likely mean all you're going to get for a job is more retail or fast food experience.

The bottom line?

A college diploma is not nearly enough to guarantee you a job. It's just the ante to get you into the game.

You have to have it or you don't stand a chance.

WAKE UP CALL #7 - Summer vacation is over.

Summers are not made for your enjoyment.

Grow up.

If you are on the track to complete school in four years, that means you have three solid summers to set yourself apart from your peer group.

Do you think an employer at your dream job is going to gush about your family travels to Italy?

As in,

"My God, I was going to hire this other applicant who spent his summers acquiring skills and demonstrating a work ethic, but you're telling me you went to Italy with your folks? That's so awesome."

Now, I'm not saying you have to go work in the salt mines all summer to prove a point, but your summer choices need to reflect your desire to both improve your skill set and develop your work ethic and character.

This issue is near and dear to me as I run one of the largest student internship programs in the country.

Our participants are absolutely committed to learning specific and marketable skills while working harder in the spring and summer than most of their future competitors.

They get it.

But what they also get (because we teach it) is that you can work hard and still have a lot of fun while you do it.

The trade off is not necessarily about fun vs. work during your summer.

It's about finding the fit for yourself so that your summer is spent in a meaningful activity that not only looks good on a resume but, most importantly, adds to your skill set.

Figuring out how working hard can be a lot of fun is that added benefit that will serve you for your entire career.

I can't hire all of you, so you will need to find that fit for yourself in the job market.

WAKE UP CALL #8 - Never take summer school.

This is where I lose friends at the campus career center and alienate parents.

It is my philosophy that you should never take summer school.

My reasons are clear: the summer must be used to differentiate yourself from your competitors in the high stakes job search right around the corner.

You are in a high stakes race to a finish line where the winners get to choose from multiple career offers and the loser gets to work at the Cheesecake Factory.

Think about it.

If you go to summer school you are able to say to a recruiter:

"Not only did I go to college, but I also went to college."

Wow, what a sales tool!

Sounds logical, so why will you ignore my advice?

Lame Excuse #1 – So you can graduate on time. On time for what? Last I checked there are no bonus points for getting out of college in four years.

Also, if you graduate "on time" without **significant prior experience**, what are you on time for?

Sitting on the couch in your parent's basement while you pretend to look for a job?

Lame Excuse #2 – Summer school will save me (or my parents) money. This is often true, however, the logic is the same as above. If you "save" money by taking summer school, you will enter the job market without **significant prior experience**.

Then what?

Spend a couple of years in a low-paying job, leeching off your parents as part of the boomerang generation?

Remember, 80% of college grads in 2009 ended up living back with their parents! Do you want to be one of them?

Lame Excuse #3 – Summer school is easier and it will improve my GPA. No one cares about your GPA. In the job market, it's about what can you do and what have you done.

GPA can be important if you lack **significant prior experience** because employers have to rely on that to figure out if you can do anything.

The thing is that the market has changed and these employers can hire from the tens of thousands of people who have 2-5 years of direct industry experience.

The only real exception to this is when/if you want to apply to grad school. If that's your deal, then suck it up and work harder during the regular school year to raise your grades.

Remember, grad schools care if you have **significant prior experience**, too.

Lame Excuse #4 – My parents are making me.

Grow up.

Pay your own way if you have to.

Which reminds me….

WAKE UP CALL #9 - You are not a kid anymore...so stop acting like one.

25 is not the new 18.

It's just that there are a lot more really lame 25 year olds in the world.

Part of the knock against the generation now entering the work force is that they never grew up.

That they are coddled adolescents who think nothing of leeching off mom and dad well into their 20s, even into their 30s.

Again, 80% of college grads in 2009 live with their parents.

It happens so often, there is even a term for it – boomerangers.

These are people who leave the nest, try to make their way in the real world, find themselves completely unprepared and incapable, and then come crawling back to Mom and Dad, hoping their old bedroom hasn't been turned into an exercise room.

Back in the old days these people were called losers.

Now they are trying to find themselves. They are searchers trying to find their niche. They are rebels who buck the system, refusing to buy into corporate America and instead seek out ways to impact the world...

...as long as Mom and Dad have a big screen TV, don't charge rent and buy their favorite cereal to eat while they play Xbox all night.

OK – loser might be a little harsh, certainly there are times when a family support structure is great and even needed when times get tough.

However, I think you and I both know that most of these folks need to grow up and take more responsibility for themselves.

Let's take you for example:

Do you pay your own way through school?

Do you pay for your own car, insurance, groceries, etc?

If not, could you help out more financially by taking a job or two during college?

Do you find yourself thinking, "But I'm young and I should be having fun instead of working?"

There is no parental code that says your parents owe you anything beyond their unconditional love and emotional support.

Anything over that is gravy.

And while gravy sure is tasty, it also clogs up your arteries and will eventually kill you.

Same thing with excessive parental help after the age of 18.

- If you seek your parent's permission instead of advice, consider that it might be time for you to grow up.

- If you live outside your means and need parental financial support to make it work, change how you live and consider that it might be time for you to grow up.

- If you think summers are for fun and you find yourself asking where your parents are going to take you this year, consider that it might be time for you to grow up.

- If the thought of paying rent to your parents if you have to move back in with them seems "unfair" to you, consider that it might be time for you to grow up.

- If you still worry about "getting in trouble" with your parents, consider that it might be time for you to grow up.

The world thinks you are part of generation too beholden to their parents, too quick to shirk responsibility and too obsessed with consumerism to make it.

Prove them wrong.....

Grow up.

WAKE UP CALL #10 - The traditional job search is dead.

It's amazing how many job seekers still begin their search by grabbing the Sunday paper and digging through the ads.

These are the worse jobs out there.

Entry-level, soul-sucking, back-of-the-bus, last-in-line, wanna-be jobs that are so bad that the recruiter cast the widest net possible in order to fill it.

And don't fool yourself thinking you're that much better because you're searching online instead of in a newspaper.

Online ads are the same jobs...only online!

The next worse jobs are found at your college career center.

This is not at all because your career center is leading you astray.

In fact, career centers are amazing resources for you if you take the time to understand what they can offer.

However, they are limited by what companies have on offer and nowadays the offerings are slim.

Companies typically go to campuses with entry-level, cookie-cutter positions.

However, even these are harder to come by now that these same employers can choose industry people with **significant prior experience** to take that same job.

Your first career job is too important to rely on the right companies just happening to show up at your campus.

What are the chances that out of the hundreds of thousands of companies out there, your perfect fit just happens to recruit at your school?

I'm not saying they don't, but the idea here is not to take the best available...but to be proactive and find the best job out there that matches your skills and goals.

The best jobs are never advertised anywhere and are impossible to find. These are exactly the jobs I'm going to teach you how to get.

WAKE UP CALL #11 - Locating a great job doesn't mean you can (or should) get it.

It is a young person's fantasy that if they could just "get a foot in the door" at their dream job then they would have it made.

Look, the world is full of people with cool and interesting jobs.

Let's take the film industry, for example.

All the people in the industry know people who want to also work in movies, but they don't go around hiring all their friends and kids of friends to be vice-presidents and studio executives.

Why?

Because successful people are usually smart, and smart people do not hire unproven people without **significant prior experience** for positions of responsibility.

So, I can (and will) teach you how to get your foot in any door, but whether you have the talent, skill and work ethic to stay in the room is up to you.

And this leads to the most important Wake Up Call of all...

WAKE UP CALL #12 - Your natural ability is not enough to get you what you want.

Sorry...but it's not.

Now, you might disagree with me. Frankly, it wouldn't surprise me if you did.

Years of constant positive affirmations (participation ribbons at sporting events, praise for C's if you 'tried hard', etc.) have likely taken their toll and you probably truly believe you have come pre-equipped for success if only you have the right opportunity.

 Poor you.

It's going to be bumpy road.

The truth is, you may very well have all the raw ingredients to be a very talented and successful (insert your career goal here), but there is a gap between your expectations and the reality of the world.

Your expectation might be that you can take what you learned in class and your concepts of hard work and, once you graduate, simply explode into your career, your superhero cape billowing in the wind behind you.

The reality is:

1) You're not even going to get into this job market without **significant prior experience**, let alone excel in it.

2) If you do somehow get a job without **significant prior experience**, you'll soon find that you are a Hyundai on a racetrack filled with Ferraris...and you might just get driven right off the road.

3) Work ethic, stress management, team leadership, and many other essential skills are developed over time and are not a switch you can turn on. Unless you have **significant prior experience**, all you can offer is potential. But, as a recruiter, why would I want to take a risk on potential when I can hire someone with a proven track record instead?

If you are serious about your goals, then you have to commit to the hard work to get it.

The world has more talkers than doers.

Time to figure out which group you are in.

READY FOR SOME GOOD NEWS?

Somehow, some way, you need to:

1) Turn yourself into a highly employable superpower before you graduate. (As you may have guessed, acquiring **significant prior experience** factors into the equation.)

2) Execute a flawless job search utilizing an out-of-the-box approach to find hidden, unadvertised jobs that are perfect for you.

3) Present yourself brilliantly so that job offers ensue.

4) Exceed everyone's expectations once you start the job.

5) Live happily ever after.

So, what's the good news?

I'm going to show you how to accomplish #1-4 in a simple, step-by-step system that worked for me and for thousands of others with whom I have shared these techniques.

If you take the advice and apply yourself to it, you will have the success and the career start you want.

In fact, I'd like to hear your success story. Come visit me at www.jeffgunhus.com and tell me all about it.

But, be warned, success isn't something you can read about, snap your fingers and *voila*, the world rolls out the red carpet for you.

It takes hard work, perseverance through adversity and a great game plan.

All I'm going to do is give you the game plan. From there, it's going to be up to you. So, if you think you're up for it, let's get started.

WAKE UP CALLS — 12 Inconvenient Truths You Should Know

#1.   The world has changed. It's tough now and it's going to get worse.

#2.   The negative impact of graduating into a bad economy will last for the first 10-15 years of your career.

#3.   Employers are done kissing up to you.

#4.   Your career will define who you are.

#5.   You need to go college (if you are currently in college, read this in case you get dumb some day and think about dropping out).

#6.   A college degree doesn't do anything for you.

#7.   Summer vacation is over.

#8.   Never take summer school.

#9.   You are not a kid anymore...so stop acting like one.

#10.   The traditional job search is dead.

#11.   Locating a great job doesn't mean you can (or should) get it.

#12.   Your natural ability is not enough to get you what you want.

CHAPTER TWO

LIPSTICK ON A PIG – HOW MOST COLLEGE GRADS THINK THEY WILL FOOL THE MARKET

Let's face it, you're a pretty good catch for a recruiter, right?

I mean, you're talented, hard working, motivated. Whenever you apply yourself to something, you excel at it.

Any employer would hire you if they only knew the <u>real</u> you.

If they would just give you a chance.

The problem is that the real world doesn't care who the real you is.

All the real world cares about is the "you" that can be proven on a resume and in person.

A little self-awareness can go a long way. Most students fail to understand how unprepared they are for the real world...until it's too late.

ARE YOU READY TO BE IN THE CAREER MARKET?

Assess for yourself: YES   NO

1. Are you nervous that you do not have   ☐   ☐
    enough work experience?

2. Does your resume stretch your work   ☐   ☐
    experience to sound more impressive
    than it really is? (Pizza delivery =
    responsible for Just-In-Time delivery
    of high quality food merchandise
    directly to the end-user.)

3. Can you illustrate your work ethic,   ☐   ☐
    tenacity and ingenuity with tangible
    examples that will be different from
    other recent college graduates?

4. Do you think your resume truly stands   ☐   ☐
    out and does not blend in with other
    candidates?

5. If you have a lot of self-confidence, will a recruiter be able to understand why once they read your resume? ☐ ☐

6. If you have exceptional plans for your career, have you shown a pattern of exceptional behavior? ☐ ☐

Some of these questions can be difficult to answer honestly. Everyone likes to believe that they are exceptional. It can be hard to admit that you may not yet have tangibly demonstrated the character traits that you feel best describe you.

This does not mean that you do not possess these traits, it only means that you can't prove them.

Some students argue that these questions are unfair.

They give me a variety of reasons why they are different and why the questions above are not necessarily an indication of their readiness for the job market.

Here are some of the common complaints and common employer answers.

1. **If the recruiter only knew the real me, I'd have the job.** If the real you hasn't done anything exceptional so far, why should I believe the *new* real you will be any different?

2. **I haven't had the opportunity to prove myself.** I stare at a stack of resumes all day from people who have done exceptional things. They have the same opportunities as you, but they chose to pursue challenge while you only did enough to get by. Nothing stopped you from paying for your own education or getting solid work experience during your summers.

3. **Good grades are not the best indication of talent.** The only problem is that the best candidates for the best jobs have great grades, were active in extracurriculars, have strong leadership skills, *and* have significant work experience.

Suppose you sit down with me for an interview with my company. My position requires a strong entrepreneurial work ethic, problem solving abilities and great communication skills. Most importantly, it is a management position where you will direct a team of 8-10 of my employees.

You might be the absolute perfect hire for this position. Heck, you might be God's gift to my company.

The problem is that unless you can dig up something you have done in your past that *specifically proves* you have the skills to do the job, you and I are not going to have much to discuss.

Over and over, the #1 mistake I see made by job applicants is that they lack the ability to make a case for themselves simply because they lack evidence of their abilities.

Going into interviews with a marginal resume is like being on trial for a crime you didn't commit.

If you don't have evidence to exonerate you, all you can do is rely on character witnesses to testify that you are a great person.

After that, you can take the stand in your own defense, without an alibi, and you make your best case that you're innocent.

You're best case is that you are a good person. The jury should just "trust you."

I see this all the time in interviews.

Faced with a perfect job opportunity, candidates squirm in their chair, speaking a mile a minute about all the potential they have, character traits they would bring to the job.

All they are doing is describing <u>what they will do</u> instead of <u>what they have done</u>.

They are asking me to "trust" that they can pull it off.

Hopefully, you got the WAKE UP CALL from Chapter One and you're already thinking what I'm thinking – employers don't need to trust that you might be able to pull off the job. They can just pick and choose from the thousands of people who have ***significant prior experience*** doing the exact job for which they are hiring.

So, here's the deal.

Finding a great job, especially in a down economy, is all about marketing and selling a product...you.

I am going to show you how tap into the hidden job market and get an awesome position.

I am going to show you how to create an amazing resume and ace any interview you do.

What I can't do is teach you how to lie.

All the systems and techniques in this book rely on one vital fact:

YOU HAVE TO TURN YOURSELF INTO A VALUABLE PRODUCT BEFORE WE CAN SELL YOU.

Or, as my family from Iowa would say, "You can slap lipstick on a pig, but it doesn't necessarily mean you'd want to kiss her." (Yeah, the word "necessarily" bothers me, too.)

GET OUT YOUR LIPSTICK

As you approach the job market, I want you to think seriously about the past experiences you have racked up in your short life that have turned you into the person you are today.

A couple of quick ones:

1. Describe three instances where you have demonstrated a strong work ethic over a long period of time.

2. Describe experiences you have had which directly mirror the responsibilities for the job to which you are applying.

3. Describe three actions/activities in your life that clearly set you apart from your peers in terms of integrity, perseverance and/or achievement.

Go ahead, write the answers down. I've provided some blank pages at the back of this book for you. I'll wait.

How did you do?

If you are like 95% of the applicants to my program, you just used a whole box of lipstick answering those questions.

Some of my favorite (real) answers I have received in interviews:

- There is this game called Halo. My buddy and I played it for 8-10 hrs a day all summer long because we were dedicated to becoming the best Halo players ever.

- My parents gave me chores to do around the house and I was always very good about getting my chores done.

- When I was a waiter at this restaurant, I would volunteer to cover shifts whenever the restaurant was short handed.

- My parents took me on a vacation for 6 weeks through Italy and they put me in charge of the travel arrangements.

OK, so these are some of the lamest attempts I faced, but the sad thing is that these answers are not far off the average!

These three simple questions really boil down to one big question:

What in your past will prove to me that you can do this job?

Unless you can nail this with an answer so specific and tangible that you would be a no-brainer for an interviewer, we have work to do before we can get into packaging and marketing you, let alone start talking about how to get into the hidden job market.

We have to create a better you.

You may have guessed it.

The only path to get you there is through ***significant prior experience***.

CHAPTER THREE

TURN YOURSELF INTO A BETTER PRODUCT...BECAUSE RIGHT NOW YOU'RE JUST NOT GOOD ENOUGH

BUILD YOUR EXPERIENCE BASE...FAST

There are all types of great advice out there to tell you what you should have done over the last four years to prepare for your career.

Learn three languages, take computer classes, intern as a freshman, and other not-at-all-helpful bits of wisdom.

But there are some things that you can do right now to help yourself be more appealing to employers.

1. **Be a joiner.** Everyone joins everything on campus. The only time club associations are a point of interest on a resume is when they are absent. A recruiter wants to know that you are active and social. If you are out of school, join professional groups in your industry of interest

2. **Be a leader.** Once you join everything, volunteer for any leadership role that is available. Leadership skills are always in demand and active leadership roles are tangible proof. Even if your 'leadership' role is to type the minutes from the meetings, it looks better than a blank space on a resume.

3. **Organize an event.** It can be anything. A charity fundraiser, a speaker for a group, a concert. Whatever it is, make it something you can point to with pride during an interview that shows initiative and innovation.

4. **Do a meaningful internship.** THE best way to help yourself.

INTERN YOUR WAY TO THE TOP

A great internship will change your life.

Obviously, I am a great believer in internship programs, since my business, College Works Painting, is one of the largest student internship programs in the country. But the facts also support my case.

Remember that sobering statistic reported by the National Association of Colleges and Employers that only 19.3% of college graduates had a job at graduation? There is another piece to the puzzle...

73% of those grads who found jobs had internship experience on their resumes!

I have seen the power of intense, significant work experience, like the one we provide in our program, and how it translates into immediate career success after graduation.

In fact, before becoming an owner, I started as an intern doing the same job I now hire hundreds annually to do.

All the examples I give with the job search successes I had while in college (I never applied for a job or did an informational meeting that did not end up yielding a job offer) were helped along by the techniques in this book, but can mostly be attributed to the fact that I had this amazing experience on my resume.

More important than the resume was the fact that I had trained myself in business during college so that when I graduated I was already at the level of someone who had been in the work force with significant management responsibility for four years.

I cannot overstate the importance of gaining experience and concrete skills during college.

You have a choice of where your starting point will be in your career.

- Either you will be another resume in the stack or you will be a stand-out.

- Either you will go into your job as a novice and go through the learning curve with everyone else, or you will have acquired skills and experiences before your first job that will allow you to excel beyond your employer's expectations.

- Either you will interview with a low-level recruiter, or you will be asked to interview with the company by someone who has already been impressed by your skills and experiences.

- Either you will talk abstractly in an interview about your character traits, or you will point to your accomplishments as concrete proof of your ability.

While these options used to mean the difference between getting a great job you love and getting a job that pays the rent, the new reality is that the difference is whether you can get a job at all!

As you ponder the way you will spend your next summer (even if it is the summer after your graduation), consider this: the 1.5 million people who graduate from college each year have two things in common.

1. They have a diploma.
2. They need a job.

Like it or not, you are one of the masses; a very small part of a very large labor pool. I'm sure that you are special and unique, but how are you going to make other people understand the intangible talents that you believe you possess?

ATTENTION WORKING STIFFS

If you are already a few years into the workforce, don't skip this chapter.

Internships are not limited to people still in school or people who do not have other jobs. Interning is a viable option at any age and at any point in a career.

There is no better way to explore new options if you are dissatisfied with your current career, or even just curious about a different one. Interning part-time while you work somewhere else can give you a safe preview of a possible career change and give you options to choose from if your current career stagnates.

If the word 'intern' bothers you, think of yourself as someone simply auditing a career just as you might audit a class at a graduate school to decide if you want to enroll.

Better to lose the ego than miss out on the opportunity to find your calling!

UNDERSTANDING INTERNSHIPS

There are a variety of internships out there from which to choose. You have to decide what type of position best fits your personality and your objective.

Before you start on your internship search, it is helpful to understand what an internship represents, both for yourself and your employer.

INTERNSHIP OBJECTIVES – THE STUDENT PERSPECTIVE

1. **Acquire skills.** This has to be the over-riding goal of the internship. Positions that provide you with exposure to an industry without creating skills are not a good investment.

2. **Career taste test.** This is the "test drive" for your career. You may have an idea of the career you want to pursue, but you really are unsure what it is all about. The internship is your chance to see what your job would be like after graduation, but also what it could be like years down the line.

3. **Make connections.** You want to surround yourself with top quality people. If you participate in a challenging, significant internship you will be doing it with like-minded individuals. As for "industry connections", I am going to teach you a better way to get those than through an internship.

4. **Build your resume**. Most resumes look very sparse right after college. It is difficult to keep a straight face as you try to explain to a recruiter that pizza delivery created a strong sense of responsibility and work ethic. Everyone

stretches past jobs to look just a little better than they were, but there is a limit. An internship finally puts some solid work experience on your resume and gets you ready to land THE job.

5. **Get school credit.** Many colleges will give you class credit for internships. Some of the procedures involve more red tape than immigrating to a new country, but it is definitely worth the effort.

6. **Do something challenging.** A challenging, significant internship is just want the doctor ordered if you want to stand out from the field.

INTERNSHIP OBJECTIVES – THE EMPLOYER PERSPECTIVE

1. **Source of cheap labor.** Many intern positions are low or non-paying positions. As a rule, the more glamorous the industry, the less pay. Classic supply and demand.

2. **Find future superstars.** The 'get them young' strategy enables companies to capture the brightest new talent in each graduating class. While this can happen, I find my Top Down Job Hunting technique to be much more effective.

3. **Reduce hiring risk**. When a company hires a new college graduate for a career position, they take a large financial risk. Training and career development will cost thousands of dollars, an investment often lost when the college grad suddenly decides the job is "just not for me." Internship programs enable the company to have a "trial run" for future employees.

4. **Help train current employees.** Internship programs often serve as a low-risk training ground for up-and-coming managers. Translation: you are red meat they can give to new managers to make mistakes on. Oh, you are going to have so much fun.

WHAT THIS MEANS TO YOU

Lucky for you, your objectives and the company objectives are a pretty good match.

They provide something you need, real life skills and exposure to an industry, and you provide them with what they need, cheap labor and a chance to discover strong talent with very little risk.

WHAT QUALIFIES AS A GOOD INTERNSHIP?

1. **A foot in the door versus getting the skills to keep you in the room.** While you might think that an internship for a prestigious firm looks great on a resume, the fact that you served coffee and made photocopies will quickly become apparent in future interviews.

   This is especially true if you intend to apply for a career job at the same company where you just interned.

   They know exactly what responsibilities their interns have. This makes it difficult to 'strengthen' (exaggerate) the internship job description in the interview. Internships should truly create strong skills and character traits that you feel will be important for your career.

A great company name on your resume may open a few doors, but if you have not invested the time to build strong skills, the door will close just as quickly.

Also, keep in mind that smaller companies often provide the best opportunities for strong internships. They are often less structured and you are more likely to be placed on meaningful projects.

2. **Your responsibilities include more than secretarial/gopher work.** If you do not choose a character-building internship, you can expect to get all of the tasks and responsibilities that no one else wants to do.

You will probably be expected to answer phones, file papers, cold call customers, make photocopies, and even pour coffee.

It's hard to argue that these are life-changing, skill-building experiences.

While you can expect to do some of these things, if they are more than 25% of your day, go find a different internship.

Make certain that you have defined projects outside of secretarial/gopher duties.

Since most internships are exactly what you do not want to do, be prepared to be an activist in defining your duties.

This means that you must have the initiative to go to your internship supervisor and suggest how you can add more value to the company.

- Is there a special project that you could do?

- Is there a significant role you could play in a presentation?

- Is there an inefficiency or a problem that no one has been able to solve because they can't afford to spend the extra time?

Bring your supervisor answers to these questions and a concrete proposal on how you would spend your time with your new duties. You might be surprised how fast you can find yourself involved in an interesting project that showcases your skills better than your previous role.

If you get resistance, offer to do these duties in addition to the other work you are already doing. Even offer to work for free!

Sound crazy?

I know that most people like to get paid for work because of that little issue of *survival,* but I'm not suggesting that you work the next six months for free, or necessarily work that many extra hours.

If you need to work a second job on the week-end to make up the extra cash, but the extra 15 hours a week at your internship creates an opportunity for you in the career of your dreams, I think you're getting a pretty good deal.

Also, most of the people who have tried this tactic usually end up getting paid for their time anyway.

Even executives feel guilty getting something for free.

3. **You have exposure to your destination job, not just the one you would have right out of college.** An internship is not only to find out what the industry is all about, but to find out what your career might be like.

Again, if you use my Top Down Job Hunting technique, you can get exposure to your career field without all the secretarial make-work projects found in most internships.

Still, if you are in an internship, the best way to see into your future is to expose yourself to as many different stages of your possible career as you can.

Talk to people who started their careers one, two, five and ten years ago.

Find out what advances they have made and what positive and negatives they can share with you. As an intern, you will have far better access to people up the food chain than you would as an employee.

If you were Joe Schmo employee in the accounting department of a major corporation and you sent a memo to the CEO requesting an informational interview "just to talk about the industry in general," the response would be lukewarm at best.

Your peers would think you were sucking up to the boss and you have to work with those people every day.

But as an intern, the same request is often seen by the CEO as a chance to influence a young person's life and is often successful.

Other interns will still think you are a suck-up, but who cares. They're just interns.

Not only that, but if you're destined for rising-stardom, there will always be a cadre of wanna-be's who will think you're a suck up.

Once again, who cares? Someday you can transfer them to the branch office in Fargo, North Dakota.

4. **You spend significant time on it.** I have interviewed applicants who spend more time explaining their internship to me than they spent doing the internship.

A 10-15 hour per week commitment may give you an understanding about the career you are trying to test-drive, but it will show you lack work ethic.

If you are still in school or working full-time to support yourself, 10-15 hours is better than sitting at home and just wondering what the inside of a hospital or a law office looks like.

But if you can, spend serious time with your internship. If you want to see what a career in the field is like, then work at your internship as if you were in the career.

Arrive early and work late.

It's the best way to get noticed and achieve your objectives.

5. **It is for a company that you may want to apply to in the future – but only if you are going in prepared to impress.** It is a common mistake for students to apply for an internship with their "dream" company before they have trained themselves to be impressive once they get there.

You get one chance to make a great impression. Don't blow yours.

HOW TO FIND THE RIGHT INTERNSHIP

The process of choosing a good internship is similar to choosing which jobs to apply for, only there is less at stake.

While your first job is a jump off of the high-dive, an internship is still in the shallow end of the pool.

Try this exercise:

1. **Take out a piece of paper and a pen and answer these questions.**

   a. **What are my goals for an internship?** Try to make them as specific as possible. If you want to become a journalist, perhaps a goal would be to get published. If you want to go into medicine, your goal might be to get exposure to an emergency room setting.

b. **What type of environment do I want to be in?** Be
    honest with yourself. Do you work well in high-
    pressure environments, or do you need something
    more subdued. If you are intent on a career that is
    high-pressure, and have never experienced that kind
    of environment before, now is the time to try it out.

c. **How serious am I about my future? What is more
    important to me, comfort or challenge?** As you do
    you research you will find some challenging
    opportunities as well as some that you could do in
    your sleep. Are you ready for a challenge? If you are
    not, what does that say about your commitment to
    your goals?

d. **Am I willing to work for free if the position gives me
    strong skills?** We are a society built on immediate
    gratification, but trust me on this one. The skills you
    will acquire from a strong internship will pay you
    back over and over again throughout your career.

    If you support yourself, find out whether loans are
    an option for you. If not, figure out how much you
    'need' to make each month and either target paid
    internships or work a 'regular' job in addition to the

internship. Is the pursuit of your passion worth not being able to afford a new car this year?

2. **Find out what opportunities exist.** Armed with your wish list for the perfect internship, use every resource available to you to find the best match.

   a. **Internship review publications.** These giant books do a good job of listing major internship programs. While they can be a little overwhelming, each has its own system of breaking down the information for you. Although reasonably priced, they can also be easily accessed at your career center. Some of the best are Princeton Review Internship Bible, Kaplan Internship Review, Adams Intern Review.

   b. **Websites.** Everything is on the Internet these days. Company home pages will often have an employment section that will include internship opportunities. If you have a company in mind, try their Website first.

   c. **Career Center.** College career centers are one of the most underutilized resources in the job search. The staff makes it their goal to know all the opportunities that are available to you. They can point you in the right direction and save you from re-inventing the wheel.

d. **Professors.** The first resource many recruiters use are the professors. They are asked to recommend any stand-outs in their classes for either career interviews or internship programs. Let your professors know that you want to be considered for any opportunities that come their way, but be certain you put yourself in a position to be someone they can confidently recommend. Use those office hours for more than arguing you should have gotten a higher grade on your paper. Start networking.

e. **Alumni.** This is the most under-utilized and under-estimated resource on campus. I never understood the power of alumni networks until I started doing interviews for my own company. If a resume comes across my desk from UC Santa Barbara, I immediately give it attention.

Strange and unfair, but I love to talk to applicants about my old school. Use your school alumni throughout your career, because they will help you.

3. **Identify and research the opportunities that interest you.**

    a. **Conduct the same research as in your job search.** Find out everything you can about the company, its products, its customers, and its future.

    b. **Evaluate your options**. Review your internship wish list. You probably are not going to find an internship that includes everything on your list, but you can get close.

    If you have difficulty deciding on what trade-offs to make, go back through your list and assign a value to each item. Once you prioritize your wish-list, your choice will become easier.

4. **Interview.**

    a. **Follow the interview guidelines discussed in this book.** The interview process will probably be less strenuous than for a career position. However, every interview needs to be approached as if it were for your dream job.

5. **Commit and shine.** Once you find the internship that meets most of your objectives, dive in head-first and commit yourself fully. Even if it turns out to be a flawed internship, use your initiative to turn it into something great.

YOUR RESPONSIBILITY

Once provided with an opportunity, it is up to you to stand out.

An internship gets your foot in the door, but what is important is what you do once you are in the room.

Take personal responsibility for your learning and for your access to the chain of command above you.

Try these tactics.

1. **Schedule an informational interview with as many people above you as possible.** Use the technique described in Top Down Job Hunting.

2. **Find mentors.** Offer to work extra hours for free on the condition that you can shadow a senior person during that time. Your eagerness to learn what someone does

gives that person a nice ego boost. It makes them excited to help you in your career.

3. **Find projects for yourself that demonstrate your skills and ingenuity.** If your internship does not give you anything challenging to do, create your own project!

4. **Industry specific projects**. Some programs require that you do a formal project during your internship. If not, do your own. Use the project as an opportunity to interview everyone important in your company and industry. This can be a useful tool when you use Top Down Job Hunting tactics.

CHARACTER BUILDING INTERNSHIPS

I reserved a separate section for a separate type of internship.

You can choose to learn anything at your own speed. For example, suppose your goal was to learn to speak Spanish. You could take seven years of a foreign language through high school and college, or you could live in the Spain for one year and completely immerse yourself in the language and the culture.

The same skill is learned, but the timeline is dramatically different.

You have the same choice about the skills and character traits you feel you will need to have in your career.

Everything can be learned over time, but why not completely immerse yourself and acquire those skills in the shortest amount of time possible?

An exercise I have my interns do is to imagine their destination job and write down what skills the person in that role would have.

Next, write down the character traits that person would need to rise to that position.

Is it a strong work ethic?

Leadership skills?

The ability to rise to a challenge?

You will find that these character traits are impossible to learn out of a book or in a classroom.

They are purely experience-based skills. You can attend every seminar in the world on leadership, and still not have a clue what you are talking about if you have never been in a leadership role.

For those impatient people who are unwilling to wait to learn these skills and character traits incrementally, there are what I call 'immersion' internships.

These are programs designed to challenge you and push you to your limits.

They create strong leadership skills and incredible self-confidence.

These internships are not for the faint of heart, but rather for people who are serious and dedicated to their futures.

My own internship program, College Works Painting, falls into this category.

I've included a description below to give you a sense of what this type of opportunity looks like.

We are only in 18 states so I can't hire all of you.

If you decide this type of internship is right for you, contact your career center and target internships that sound similar in scope.

COLLEGE WORKS PAINTING

College Works Painting is the best internship program in the world.

OK, so I am a bit biased since I am one of the owners, but it doesn't change the fact that I also think it's true.

I can say this because I actually worked my way through the ranks of College Works, starting as an intern my freshman year in college.

I experienced first-hand what our interns go through and have spent the last 18 years of my life developing and improving the experience.

Although I now own a $40 million company with thousands of employees, I still look at my first year as a College Works intern as one of my most challenging and rewarding business and leadership experiences in my life.

The program is designed to immerse you into a challenging and intense experience that pushes you leave your comfort zone and create the skill set you need to compete for any career you want in the future.

Rather than learning management and leadership skills in a classroom setting, our interns have an actual, real-world experience.

College Works interns operate a house painting business for the summer.

Interns design and implement a marketing program, conduct sales presentations, calculate estimates, recruit, hire, and train their own employees, manage customer service, quality control, production management, and cost control.

Program participants attend a thorough training program and work hand-in-hand with a mentor. It is a paid internship with the average intern earning $6,700 over the summer and top interns earning well over $20,000.

Obviously, this program has nothing to do with painting houses.

A painting business is simply the tool we use to teach our interns the character traits that are inherent in entrepreneurs and leaders. These skills translate into any number of career fields.

Many of our interns have no intention of pursuing a career in business, but recognize the need to build strong leadership skills for the field they want to pursue.

Our interns do not want to go on to become middle managers, they want to be CEOs.

They do not want to be surgeons; they want to be chiefs-of-surgery.

They do not want to be stockbrokers; they want to be hedge-fund managers.

They do not want to be engineers; they want to be project leaders.

The College Works program instills the values and character traits necessary to achieve this kind of success.

The program is designed to give interns a realistic experience as an entrepreneur, but it's essentially the real world with a safety net.

First year participants are taken through extensive training and are provided a mentor to walk them through the learning curve. The College Works program forces interns to deal with situations and problems that most people do not have to face until they are well into their careers.

It is designed for people who are eager to get the skills early so that they can set themselves apart from their peers.

Past interns describe their experience as difficult, challenging, and one of the most important experiences that shaped their career success.

Connections

The people that you meet through a character-building internship are just as important as the skills that you learn from the program.

Everyone you meet is intent on achieving something great in their life and they are impatient to do it. These are great people to know and to hang out with.

Although I had great friends in my social circle in college, their goals usually centered on beer consumption.

In comparison, my College Works summer introduced me to my four business partners, as well as over ten other people who currently run multi-million dollar businesses. I continue to meet exceptional talent every year that I run this program.

College Works provides an extensive alumni network of young professionals and entrepreneurs to assist top interns in their careers after they complete the program.

Our alumni understand what it takes to be successful at this program and are more than willing to recommend, and in many cases, hire College Works interns.

The most successful interns will be invited to continue with the company for the rest of their time in college and potentially full time as a career once they graduate.

There exist several opportunities within College Works and our parent company, National Services Group.

These opportunities range from management, finance, and accounting, to sales, marketing, and human relations.

All senior management positions in my different companies are held by past College Works interns.

How to Apply:

College Works admissions run from the fall quarter/semester to the end of March. Current states include California, Colorado, Wyoming, Utah, Washington, Oregon, Arizona, Texas, Missouri, Kansas, Illinois, Michigan, Pennsylvania, Massachusetts, Connecticut, Virginia, Maryland and Ohio.

Admissions are very selective with only one in ten applicants accepted to the program. The selection process includes an initial screening interview and two formal interviews with senior management. A resume, application, and strong personal references are required.

Call or write to:
COLLEGE WORKS PAINTING
1682 Langley Avenue
Irvine, CA 92617
(888) 450-9675
(800) 394-6000
Email: info@collegeworks.com
Web: www.collegeworks.com

COP-OUTS – EXCUSES YOU'LL USE TO GET OUT OF DOING A CHALLENGING INTERNSHIP.

It's too late. I'm graduating soon and I need to find a job. It is never too late to do an internship or take a new direction. Even a few years after graduation, internships are the best way to preview your career. I have recommended to several college graduates that they intern for the summer after their graduation rather than take a low paying job outside their industry.

I have plenty of time before I graduate. I'm taking the summer off. Everyone thinks they have a lot of time before they have to start planning for a career. Then you wake up one day wearing a graduation gown and someone putting a diploma in your hand.

Congratulations, now go find an employer excited about someone with no tangible skills.

Review WAKE UP CALL #8 and grow up a little. Summer vacation is over. It's time to get to work.

I need to take summer school to graduate on time. Go back and read WAKE UP CALL #9. If you still don't buy it, there's not much I can do for you. I'm sorry you wasted your money buying this book.

No resume or interview advice in the world is going to save you from having to say, "Not only did I go to school, but I also went to school."

TOP REASONS WHY GOOD PEOPLE DO BAD INTERNSHIPS.

1. **Family Friend/Parents.** Your parents are so eager to see their son/daughter get a great job that they are more than happy to take care of your career choice for you. One day you are informed that you have an internship "blind date" with a family friend. While this could potentially be a great opportunity, it often backfires.

   a. It is usually in a field where your parents picture you, not where you picture yourself.

   b. The family friend feels obligated to offer you the internship as a favor, but is unsure what to do with you. They create make-work projects just to get you out of their hair.

   c. If the internship does not work out, you are certain to offend someone, usually your parents.

2. **Family Business.** While a job with the family business may actually give you more responsibilities than many positions, recruiters sometimes discount resumes with too much family business experience. It is assumed that

allowances are made for family members that a regular employee would not receive.

Also, the experiences tend to be exaggerated and difficult to check. (It's hard to find out about someone's past job experience when their old boss is their mom.) While some family businesses are harder on relatives than regular employees, it is hard for a recruiter to know for sure. Make certain that you have experience outside the family business.

3. **Designer Internships.** Do not be lured in by prestigious or popular brand name internships. Evaluate the internship based on its merit, not just the company name.

   An internship at some posh corporate headquarters where you make copies all day still only teaches you how to run a copier.

   Entering the job market without strong work experience is a scary proposition. It often lowers the confidence level of first-time career hunters and causes them to lower their sights and accept dead-end positions.

4. **Lack Of Research.** You know that you should get an internship. Everyone else has one, so you jump on the

wagon. After you look through the campus newspaper and circle every ad that has the word 'intern' in it, you send out a few resumes, get a few offers, and choose the company that will be the easiest commute.

Suddenly, you are an unpaid receptionist in the middle of an office full of people playing a great game called, "give it to the intern."

GRAD SCHOOL ANYONE?

Now that we have spent all this time on how to acquire practical, real world skills, let's talk briefly about how to evade the real world for a few more years. I am, of course, talking about graduate school.

The thought of grad school usually makes people react in one of two ways, either relief or massive depression.

Relief because it signals a respite from the reality of a nine-to-five job, mean bosses, idiot co-workers, commuting, and all of those other grown-up accessories.

Massive depression at the thought of putting your life back on hold so that you can listen to overpaid professors wax philosophically how they would change the world while you add another pile of money to your already monstrous student loans.

Before you discount grad school, listen to this statistic.

For the first time in U.S. history, race and gender are no longer the greatest indicators of economic prosperity. The new leading indicator is education.

There is a proven correlation between the level of education someone accumulates and their economic well-being.

Money certainly isn't the key to fulfillment, but advanced education can create greater opportunities for advancement, control of your environment, and open doors that you didn't know existed.

So when is it a good time, if ever, to go back to grad school?

The answer really depends on your particular field and what you are trying to accomplish in it.

For example, if your passion is child psychology and you want to open your own practice, it's not too difficult to figure out that you need additional education.

On the other hand, if you are starting a business career it may be less clear whether you should shell out the money for an MBA or not. It is a tricky decision, but here are some thoughts that may make it a bit easier.

1. **Make an educated decision.** Be as thorough about deciding to go to grad school as you are about choosing a career. Consult everyone that could have an opinion and weigh all of your options.

2. **Understand the return on your investment.** Find out from people in the field what benefits an advanced degree would give you. Interview people who have been successful with and without the extra credentials.

3. **Think long-term.** Two years of graduate school may seem like an eternity right now, but it's a blink of the eye in the grand scheme of things. If the long-term impact of an advanced degree would be two or three decades of more interesting and rewarding career opportunities, wouldn't it be worth it?

4. **Go for the right reasons.** Missing the college social scene and being tired of working (after your first six months of your first job) do not qualify. Graduate school can be an excellent avenue if your field requires it for advancement, you feel the investment will equip you with the skills you need to achieve your goals, or because you are passionate about acquiring more knowledge about your field.

5. **Be careful not to become a professional student.** I had a friend in college who was on her fourth Masters degree, all in very different areas. While she was well-versed in subjects ranging from the mating habits of the North America bison to the impact of depreciating capital goods on an income statement, she had no intention of really *doing* anything. She loved hanging out on campus and living the student lifestyle and taking classes just gave her a good reason to stay around. Watch out for the professional student trap. If you go back to school do so with a mission in mind.

6. **Consider night classes.** Many good graduate programs cater to professionals by offering night or week-end courses. This would enable you to acquire your additional credentials while you continue to get an inside look at the career field you have chosen.

Ultimately, there is no such thing as too much education. You will never catch yourself later in your life thinking,

"Boy, I really wish I didn't have this Masters degree hanging over my head."

However, there are other ways to be a life-long learner and advance your knowledge of your field. Seminars, speaker programs, community classes, and professional organizations can provide you with educational opportunities specific to your field.

The decision to enter a graduate program can be a pivotal point in your career progress, but it entirely depends on your field and your objectives. Seek out advice from those around you and do some serious soul-searching before you jump to a conclusion.

THE LAST WORD

- With the new reality, ***significant prior experience*** is more important than ever.

- Don't fall into the trap of getting a "summer job" to pay the bills. That is no longer good enough.

- Use your summers to turn yourself into a marketable asset.

Before you read this book, what was the summer job you were thinking about doing?

Even after everything you just learned, I bet there is a 90% chance you'll still work in that same job.

It's human nature to stay in your comfort zone.

Buck the trend. Be different. Don't just get a job this summer. Change your life instead.

CHAPTER FOUR

STRUT YOUR STUFF – Resumes and Cover Letters

So, hopefully you bought in that you need to get **_significant prior experience_** in order to be competitive in the new reality.

Once you get this experience, we can then package you and sell you creatively through the Top Down Job Hunting method.

However, both to get this **_significant prior experience_** and to successfully navigate Top Down Job Hunting, we need to get your marketing materials in the best shape we can.

A career search is like going into battle.

Like most battles, the outcome will be determined by not only your skill, but also by the weapons at your disposal. In this case, your weapons are the marketing tools that let employers know who you are and what you can do.

There is a saying that if you build a better mousetrap, the world will beat a path to your door. In today's economy, the most successful mousetrap company not only has to have a better product but also have a better advertising campaign.

Marketing sells.

Unless you can get yourself into the interview and ultimately into the job you want, you will never have the opportunity to prove yourself.

We need to work together to create tools and strategies to give you the best opportunity possible to get that job and have that chance.

However, remember that marketing can only do so much.

I might buy a mousetrap because of a great advertising campaign, but if it doesn't work, I'll never buy the same brand again.

We are going to get you in the door, but you have to perform well enough to stay in the room!

HOW TO WRITE THE BEST RESUME IN THE WORLD

OK, so maybe that's false advertising. There is really only one way to write a truly great resume...have ***significant prior experience*** to put on there.

However, this section will help you to write the most powerful resume your experience will allow.

 It will cover the basics and some important tricks of the trade that can mean the difference between an effective resume and trash can fodder. If you want more information on resumes, I highly recommend your campus career center which will typically offer workshops on the subject.

There is a standard resume format that recruiters want to see.

They have to look at thousands of resumes and they have a very low tolerance for anything out of the ordinary, especially if it makes the resume difficult to read. (For you die-hard rule breakers, check out the Creative Options section at the end of this chapter.) I understand that you want to show how individualistic you are, but I recommend that you pick a different time to do it. Your effort to stand out might get you thrown out.

THE BASICS

1. **Type and Font.** Resumes need to be 12 point and a neutral font.

2. **Paper.** Use a high quality, white or light cream paper. A 40 to 70 pound paper is perfect. Do not get fancy with marbled or shaded paper.

3. **Style.** Never use italics as they are hard to read. Use capitalization and bold to highlight items.

4. **Length.** One page and one page only. There is nothing so important in your career that would require two pages.

5. **No personal pronouns or abbreviations.** For you math majors, those are words like I, he, she, you.

6. **Never fold a resume.** If you mail a resume, use an 8.5 x 11 envelope.

THE SEVEN RESUME RULES

1. **<u>Perfection.</u>** Nothing less than perfection is acceptable on a resume. This document is your absolutely best foot forward. Your big chance to prove you can be a professional. Any error in the document is a massive strike against you. Check for spelling errors at least a thousand times and have it proof-read by half of the English department. Be consistent with your verb tenses and avoid grammatical errors.

2. **Visually appealing.** Your document needs to reflect the effort you put into it. It should be easy to read and well designed. A simple test: turn your resume upside-down and see what you think. It's surprising how much easier it is to see the balance of the page when you are not focusing on the words.

3. **Concise and easy to understand.** Your reader needs to easily pick out the information they want and never have to read it twice. If your proofreader asks for a clarification, take that as a sign that you need to change something on your resume.

4.   **Don't overstate your skills.** Put your best foot forward when describing your past jobs, but if you exaggerate you will ruin your credibility.

5.   **Never lie.** People get caught in the most ridiculous lies all the time. Employers <u>will</u> check your past employment, your academic records and your references.

If there is something about you that you think will be a deal breaker with a recruiter, take the bull by the horns and explain it directly to them in the interview.

If your GPA is in the basement, don't include it. If your overall GPA is bad, calculate your major GPA and use that if the number looks good. If you have a poor GPA and it comes up in the interview, offer an explanation and follow-up with why you think you would still be a good risk despite your academic shortcomings.

6. **Tailored.** Your resume needs to be tailored to each interview you attend. The recruiter will appreciate the effort and it will get the interview off to a strong start. If you do not have access to a computer, print out some different versions that you can use for different interviews.

7. **Current contact information.** If you are about to move, list a permanent address and phone number. Do not overload the recruiter with too many numbers and make certain the phone numbers you give will be properly answered. There is nothing better than the recruiter from Goldman Sachs calling from New York and your fraternity brother answering the phone with a belch.

THE FORMAT

If you looked through a pile of one hundred resumes you would see one hundred different styles.

However, there would be some resumes that automatically stand out because they are well formatted and seem easy to read.

There is no 100% correct way to write a resume, but there are conventions that serve as a good guide.

First, your name and current contact information are at the top of the page. Include an e-mail address (and please make it professional...if your email address is thehotness@aol.com get a new address for your job search.) You can center this information or block it into a corner.

Look at some sample resumes at www.thecareerseries.com to see what style you prefer.

Your basic subject headings:

- Objective
- Summary
- Education
- Work Experience
- Activities/Interests
- Skills

WRITE AN INCREDIBLE OBJECTIVE STATEMENT

You have a very short time to grab your reader's attention. The near-perfection of your typesetting is a start, but the Objective is your first line of defense.

The Objective is a concise statement to tell the employer about your immediate career goal.

It allows you to directly communicate your purpose for pursuing the position in a well thought out and clear manner.

Just make certain that it is well thought out and clear. I have read some long, confusing objective statements that only served to distract me from the interview. Keep it short and sweet.

A good trick is to read it out loud.

If you could use your objective as an answer to an interview question, then you are in good shape.

If you sound like you are reading Chapters One and Two of a Charles Dickens novel, you might need a little more work.

Try this formula for your Objective.

1. List the job in which you are interested. (Accountant, Architect, Programmer)

2. List the industry. (Computer, Entertainment, Construction)

3. Indicate the geographical areas that interest you.

Examples:

- Staff accountant in the Entertainment industry in the Los Angeles area.

- Graphic Design Artist for a major daily newspaper-open to relocation.

- Marketing position with major sports team-open to relocation and travel.

BEWARE OF THE THESAURUS

These Objectives listed above are concise and tell the reader exactly what you want. Most Objectives that I read are long-winded paragraph-sized sentences with gigantic words. These two sentences say basically the same thing. Which one makes more sense?

Objective: Management position in a dynamic, growth-oriented company with strong opportunities for advancement.

Objective: To pursue a career path utilizing abstract thought process in the development of lasting team dynamics and interdepartmental synergies.

I don't even know what the second one *means.*

Leave the thesaurus in your desk. An Objective statement is not the one sentence proof that you passed English 101. It needs to be clear, concise and simple. You are best served by always writing as you would speak to someone.

If you regularly talk about 'interdepartmental synergies' then feel free to let loose. Otherwise, use clear language to communicate your career intentions to the reader.

DO I REALLY NEED AN OBJECTIVE?

The Objective is not optional. Do not let someone tell you that it is because you will hurt yourself by not including one on your resume.

Some say that it limits your opportunities because you are narrowing your job search.

Yes, that is the point.

You are communicating to the resume reader that you are a viable candidate for their position because your goals match with the opportunity they have to fill.

If you are worried about having too narrow a focus then you can have different Objectives for different resumes if you are unsure of what you truly want. In any case, make certain that you have an Objective on every resume that you send out.

SUMMARY - THE MOST IMPORTANT PART OF THE RESUME THAT YOU'LL FORGET TO DO.

The Summary is my favorite part of the resume.

It is a quick snapshot of the candidate written in easy to understand language and designed to give me a lot of information in a short amount of time.

A well-written Summary will point out important attributes or accomplishments of the candidate, explain how these relate to the position in question, and encourage me to read through the rest of the resume.

This is where I like to see the **_significant prior experience_** highlighted. It tells me I should pay attention to the rest of the resume.

Surprisingly, most of the resumes I read do not have a Summary.

Without a Summary, the candidate is relying on my patience to read the entire resume and pick out the most important points for myself.

Because of my incredible lack of patience, I seldom read a resume, but rather quickly scan the resume to pick out relevant points.

Therefore, a resume without a Summary is relying on the most important points being seen during a 15-20 second scan of the page.

I don't know about you, but I don't like those odds.

WHAT TO INCLUDE

The Summary is a bullet-pointed highlight film of the resume about to follow. It allows that recruiter to quickly identify the relevant experiences you have accumulated and enables you to draw attention to your greatest accomplishments.

- Three or four bullet points.

- Emphasizes past accomplishments relevant to position.

- Concrete facts, nothing glossy or abstract.

- Concise. The details are contained in the resume.

This is your 15-second commercial about yourself.

It has to convince the reader that it is worth their time to read the rest of the resume.

Imagine that the recruiter is only going to read the Summary from your resume. (It often happens that way.)

Is your Summary enticing enough to make the recruiter want to talk to you? If not, try again.

EDUCATION

List the school you attended and the degrees you have earned or currently have in progress. List the most advanced degree first. Include your graduation date or your projected date.

Only include a GPA if it is something to brag about. Otherwise keep that little bit of information to yourself until you can win the employer over in the interview.

Also, do not assume that the recruiter will understand abbreviations. USD can be the University of San Diego or the University of South Dakota.

WORK EXPERIENCE

List all of your relevant work experience in reverse chronological order, with your most recent job first.

This is where your _significant prior experience_ gets to shine.

Include your employer's name, the dates you worked, and your responsibilities. Make sure that you explain any gaps in your work history. This is your opportunity to showcase all of those long hours of training that prepared you to be a high-achiever in your field.

When I conduct interviews, work experience is the first area I study and where I form my first impression of the candidate.

I give a quick glance to the company name and go right for the job responsibilities. I do not care who you worked for, just tell me what you did and how that made you a good candidate for my position.

Resist the temptation to write a descriptive paragraph of everything you did in your past job. Use bullet points so it will be read. Include only the items that say the most about you and your abilities.

ACTIVITIES AND INTERESTS

Generate the laundry list of interests that you pursue in your free time. Choose the top 3-5 most interesting things to include. (An excessive activities list can be distracting and usually boring if you only have the usual "Reading, Sports, Travel.)

Try to find something interesting about yourself. If you can't, maybe you should try to get out more. Also, avoid anything too strange if you are applying to a mainstream company.

I interviewed a candidate who included role-playing games and body piercing as his activities. Hmmm.

I spend some time looking through this section when I conduct interviews. I want to see that the person is active and see if we have something in common.

A short conversation about a hobby or a sport allows me to see how the candidate reacts to a more social conversation.

Also, I look for interests that show the character traits that the candidate has used to describe herself. If she describes herself as outgoing and adventurous, I want to see that she pursues activities that reflect that. If not, I will probe more to make certain she is representing herself correctly.

Several times a year, I interview a candidate who falls apart under a simple question about a hobby.

I love the outdoors, hiking, mountain stream fishing and the like, so whenever someone has something similar on their resume I like to ask them about their favorite spots to visit.

I'm not trying to be tricky, I just like to find new places to go.

There are always a few candidates who get flustered and admit that they don't really do much outdoors, but they thought it would sound good on their resume.

Not a great first impression.

Moral of the story: don't make stuff up.

Being boring because you don't do many activities is not an interview crime, but frivolous lying can hurt your chances.

SKILLS

This is pretty straight-forward. Include specific computer skills, leadership qualities, and languages that you possess.

REFERENCE POWER

References are an incredibly important part of the job search.

The section below talks about how to use your references, but the first question is how to treat references on your resume. A classic mistake made on resumes is that they don't end, but rather just fade away.

It's like a movie where all of the action happens in the first ten minutes with the next hour and a half spent 'winding down.' This is what most resumes look like.

Here's my Objective, Summary, and great Work Experience, then some Skills, some Activities, some of this, some of that. Where is the finale?

Whatever you do, don't use "References available on request."

This is used so often that it is essentially invisible to the reader of the resume. Use this opportunity to stand out and to create a finale for your resume. Try one of these:

- Strong references available to prove outstanding work ethic and initiative.

- Strong references available to demonstrate exceptional work ethic and ambition.

- Strong references available to demonstrate exceptional creativity and work ethic.

These lines will catch the reader's eye because they are not used to finding something original at the end of the page. I recommend that you put this one sentence in bold letters to draw even more attention to it.

WHERE TO FIND INCREDIBLE REFERENCES

Your references can be an incredibly valuable tool if you use them properly.

It is amazing the number of times I have called a reference only to have the person not recommend the candidate for the position!

A reference is supposed to be your best advocate. Take the time to choose and prepare them to make sure that they will represent you well.

The quality of your references relies on the quality of the relationships you have built with people and the quality of work you have done in your past. The best candidates are:

- Past employers - especially from the same field.

- Extracurricular advisors - student government, club advisors, etc.

- Professors.

- Personal professional acquaintances - friends of the family.

- Do not include strictly personal references. (I don't want to talk to your Mom.)

You can see why it is important to cultivate relationships with your professors and employers. You want your references to attest to a pattern of behavior over a period of time.

A professor who barely knows your name and can only provide your class grade and attendance record does not do you any good.

DO A REFERENCE QUALITY CONTROL CHECK

If it bothers you that your fate might lie in the hands of your references, conduct a quality control check. Ask each of your references to write a letter of recommendation for you. This will:

1. Let you know what they will say about you.

2. Make certain that they are willing to spend the time to be a good reference.

3. Give you a valuable tool to use in the interview process.

If they need a place to start, give them a few simple questions to serve as an outline. How long have you known the candidate? What do you think of them professionally/personally? Do you feel they would be good in the _____ field? Why? Is there anything else you would like us to know about this candidate?

Ask your reference to type the letter on letterhead. Give them plenty of notice, but do ask for the letter by a particular date. This is easy to do this in an unobtrusive manner. "I have an interview in two weeks. Do you think I could come by and pick up the letter ten days from now? Will that give you enough time?"

If you do not ask for the letter by a particular date, chances are you will have to call for it a few times, making you the annoying reference-letter seeker.

Not the title you want to give yourself.

Once you have the letters of recommendation, make sure that you put them to good use. Always bring them to any interview that you attend.

At the end of the interview, offer the letters to the recruiter. You will seldom have someone decline the invitation.

Most often, the recruiter will take the short-cut and use the reference letters instead of making phone calls.

This is great because you have effectively controlled the content of your references.

You know what was said. You know that it was good.

INVOLVE YOUR REFERENCES IN THE PROCESS

You want your reference to feel like they have a stake in your success.

I love giving references for my past interns, especially the ones who did exceptionally well.

I make it my mission that they get a job offer from every recruiter who calls me.

I spend a great deal of time on the phone when a recruiter calls me. I give concrete examples that support my recommendation and make the recruiter understand the challenging nature of the position they held with my company.

I never lie and I never embellish in these calls. Mostly because it would be against my values to do so, but my interns also make it easy on me because anyone who completes my program truly has something to brag about.

Even without meeting the individual, I know anyone completing my program will have tremendous work ethic, problem-solving skills and leadership ability.

If not, they wouldn't have survived the program.

Make sure you are the kind of person whom your references can and will recommend with confidence.

Here are some ways to keep your references involved:

- Call your references whenever you give out their information to a company. Let them know that someone may call. If the interview did not go as well as you thought and no one calls, you don't look bad to your references.

- Tell them about the opportunities you interview for and ask for their input. This will prepare your references for the phone call from the recruiter and give you a chance to make your case as to why you would make a good candidate for the position.

- Ask your references for advice on what companies you should contact. Also, ask if they have a particular contact name they would recommend. "Pulling strings" is a time-honored tradition, and if your references have friends in the industry, you have a great way to get in the door.

- Send thank you letters to all of your references once you are hired. You can expect several job changes in your life, so you will need references again in the future. It's always nice to keep in touch.

FINAL RESUME TIPS

1. **Hire a professional to format your resume.** Your resume is so important, why not take it to a professional? There are many resume services and they are not very expensive. Many of the large copy chains, like Kinko's, offer a great service. It is worth the investment.

2. **Get advice on content.** Show your resume to anyone who will take the time to read it. Try your professors, your parents, your friends, your career counselors, even recruiters who are on campus to interview for a different position.

3. **Update your resume constantly.** You never know when an opportunity will jump up and demand your resume. Whenever something changes in your life, reflect it in your resume. It is always a work in progress.

Although I suggest you use a professional and/or spend time at your campus career center in a resume class, you can check out resume samples at www.jeffgunhus.com.

HOW TO WRITE THE BEST COVER LETTER IN THE WORLD

The purpose of the cover letter is to explain how you (the candidate) will benefit me (the company).

Unfortunately, 90% of cover letters are simply a paragraph form of the resume I just read.

I say "just read" because the cover letter is usually the last thing most recruiters read.

That may be surprising to you, especially because you probably have received advice in the past that the cover letter is the introduction to your resume. This is not true.

Cover letters are seldom read, unless you clear the first two parts of the screening process first.

Here is the process when a recruiter reads your resume:

1. **Scan the resume.** Look for keywords and experience. If still interested...
2. **Read the resume.** Get details about past experiences. If still interested...
3. **Read the cover letter.** This means that I am interested in the candidate and I am willing to take the time to read a hopefully well written explanation of why I should pursue the candidate for an interview.

As I read through your resume and cover letter, I am deciding where to allocate my interview time.

Your job is to make your marketing tools so effective that I choose you from the stack of resumes that pile up on my desk every day.

There are some basic marketing concepts that are important for you to understand in order for you to be successful.

ARGUE BENEFITS, NOT FEATURES

A little Sales 101. People buy benefits. It is how a product or service will help them or improve their life that makes a customer decide to buy.

Features are the descriptive characteristics of the product or service. A health club has features like new exercise equipment, a pool, a spa, and tennis courts. It also creates benefits for new members like improved health, more energy, and a good-looking body. People purchase a health club membership because they picture themselves with a model's body, not because the equipment is in good shape.

Companies follow the same logic.

Candidates are selected based on benefits, not features.

Your resume is all features; this is who I am and what I have done.

Feature, feature, feature.

The cover letter is where you sell the benefits that you represent. You don't want to rely on the interviewer's ability to draw the lines between the features you possess and how your experiences and skills fit into the requirements of the position.

Honestly, sometimes interviewers just aren't that good. Or they're tired. Or disinterested.

So why leave it to them to figure it out.

The features in your cover letter are your supporting evidence, but benefits will get you the interview.

Through your cover letter, you must convince the reader that you have skills and attributes that differentiate you from the other people applying for the same position.

It is how these skills and attributes create benefits for the recruiter that will make you a good use of the recruiter's time.

WRITING THE LETTER

The cover letter should be written in the same font as your resume and be on the same paper. Address it to the specific person who will be reading the letter. This may take a little research, but it is worth it to avoid the dreaded, "To Whom It May Concern."

The letter should be three paragraphs long.

1. The first is a specific reference to the job for which you are applying and how you can satisfy the <u>need</u> the company has expressed. Also include how you heard of the opening. If you were referred personally by someone in the company, this is the perfect opportunity for you to shamelessly drop their name. It is expected and, in fact, helpful to the person reading the letter.

2. The second paragraph is a summary of the benefits you can give the company. Use the bullet points from your summary to describe the most important features that you want the recruiter to remember about you. Follow up each feature with its consequences. That is, explain how these features translate into a benefit for the company. Limit yourself to four or five sentences, but make them good ones.

3. The third paragraph is a close. In sales, a close in a demand for action. You wrote the letter for a purpose and that is to interview for the position. Give the recruiter a specific way to contact you. Tell the employer that you will contact them on a specific day to further discuss employment opportunities if you do not hear from them by a particular date.

CREATIVE OPTIONS

1. **P.S.** If you want to grab a reader's attention, add a P.S. at the bottom of the page. It is somewhat gimmicky, but it can be effective. Make sure that you have something significant to say.

2. **References.** If you have exceptional references, the cover letter might be another way for you to use them. You can include quotes from a reference in the body on the letter, or include an entire paragraph in the middle of the letter.

   I have seen letters with quotes filling the margin surrounding the body of the letter. It looked too cluttered, but I still showed it around the office and still remember the candidate because of it. Use your creativity, but be careful not to lose your message in the fluff.

3. **Humor.** A friend of mine was turned down from every job possible in the entertainment industry. She couldn't even get an interview. As a last resort, she changed her serious reference letter to a script for a melodramatic radio drama of a poor farm girl (her) trying to make it big in the cruelty of Hollywood. It caught somebody's

attention and she landed a job reading scripts for a major production house. When she started, everyone in the office referred to her as the radio-drama girl because the recruiter had read the cover letter to everyone. Needless to say, the serious cover letters never received as much attention.

CAUTION

Humor and creativity is very subjective. Funny to one person is insulting to the next. Using humor can be your ticket in the door, but it also holds the greatest possibility of total and dismal failure. It can work, but it can also back-fire on you. Joke with care.

FINAL COVER LETTER TIPS

1. **Treat it like your resume.** Give your cover letter the same scrutiny that you gave your resume. Let everyone read it and check it for errors at least a thousand times.

2. **Get the right name.** Work hard to find out who will read your letter. If it could be one of two people interviewing, bring two copies so you will have the right name.

3. **Constantly work on it.** It can always get better. Ask more people for advice and update it with new information. It is the first thing your reader sees. It has to be perfect.

SAMPLE COVER LETTER

Mr. Michael Johnson
Los Angeles Lakers
123 Chapparel Road
Inglewood, CA 90802

October 17, 2008

Dear Mr. Johnson,

I am responding to your ad in the Sunday Los Angeles Times for "Marketing Executive – LA Lakers." My background has prepared me specifically for a career in sport marketing and I feel that I would be a valuable asset for your department.

I am a recent graduate from the University of Southern California where I majored in Marketing. Many of my professors also consult with major corporations, so I was able to gain valuable insight into the latest trends in corporate marketing. Also, I interned for the marketing department of the Long Beach Ice Dogs. This experience trained me in promotions, special events, and media contacts, giving me a strong background that will enable me to quickly learn the position with your organization.

My previous experience, strong work ethic, and proven ambition make me a strong candidate for this position. I would like to discuss this opportunity with you more thoroughly at your convenience. I will call your office at 10am on July 12 to see if we can set an appointment. If you would like to contact me before then, I can be reached at 562-434-1818.

Thank you for your time and your consideration.

Sincerely,

Amy Ginsberg

PREPARE FOR THE RESPONSE

ANSWERING MACHINES, ROOM-MATES, AND PARENTS.

Now that you have sent out your resumes, prepare yourself for the responses. Even if you did all of your research with due diligence, chances are that your resume sending activity will initially be greeted with a deafening silence.

Don't worry.

It will take a little while for you to get your first interviews. Even though you will actively attract the recruiter's attention with follow-up calls, be prepared for them to take the first step as well.

1. **Answering machines.** Change your answering machine or voicemail on your cell phone to something you would want an employer to hear. The latest techo hit thumping in the background is probably not a first impression you want to make.

2. **Roommates.** Tell your roommates that you expect an important phone call. I called a candidate once and was told by her giggling roommate that she was in the bathroom and would probably be there for a while. I didn't care, but when the candidate called back, she was obviously very embarrassed. Also, make a special message board so you don't miss an opportunity.

3. **Parents.** If you live with your parents, let them know what is going on. I once called a candidate at 10:30 on a Monday morning. His mother answered the phone and complained to me for five minutes about how lazy her son was to still be in bed. She never asked who I was.

4. **Yourself.** Be prepared for a phone call from a potential employer. Think about what you want to say and how you want to come across on the phone. Have your schedule ready so that you can come across as organized when the employer sets a time with you to interview.

THE LAST WORD

- Resumes and cover letters are representative of your best abilities. Anything less than perfection is an unforgivable shortcoming.

- Get help. Have your resume and cover letter reviewed by someone with expertise in the field. Spend the money on a resume service that will format your document professionally.

- References can be an incredible asset if they are used correctly. Conduct a quality control check to make certain that your references are working hard for you.

- Argue benefits not features in your cover letter. Features say what you've done while benefits describe how what you've done will help the employers to whom you are applying.

- Prepare to professionally handle the response from the companies you have contacted.

CHAPTER FIVE

ACE THE INTERVIEW

Whether part of your search is for the internship designed to give you ***significant prior experience*** or for the career search utilizing Top Down Job Hunting, you are going to need to be "good in the room."

All the marketing efforts and skill creation will come down to this one meeting where you have to convince the person across the table that you have what it takes to do the job.

Depending on your personality, the word "interview" either excites you because you finally have the opportunity to get in front of a living, breathing decision-maker, or it has you gasping for air as you hyper-ventilate through an anxiety attack.

Whether you have sweaty palms or cool demeanor, this chapter will prepare you to give best interview you can give.

Unfortunately, the technique I am about to teach you is typically the step job candidates are most likely to skip.

While the interview can mean the difference between getting a dream job or not, the exercises I describe in this chapter look and sound like work. But it's essential that you do it.

THE PURPOSE OF THE INTERVIEW

THE INTERVIEWER'S PERSPECTIVE

1. **Screen the applicant.** Make a quick judgment whether the applicant is even a serious candidate for the position.

2. **Evaluate the candidate.** Use the candidate's performance during the interview as a measure of

competence and ability to perform in the offered position.

3. **Convey information.** Make the candidate aware of the details of the position for which they are applying. This lays the groundwork in case the applicant is accepted for the position.

4. **Minimize risk.** An employer, especially a professional recruiter, has a lot at stake when they hire someone. They bear the responsibility if they make a poor hiring decision.

Interviewers want to protect their reputation and hire the 'sure thing.'

They want to see concrete skills and credentials, so that if you turn out to be a bad apple they have a strong justification why they hired you. When you steal your company car or sell the company secrets to a competitor, it is easier for the recruiter who hired you to say, "How could I have known? She was a Harvard MBA," than it is to weakly mumble, "Well, he seemed nice in the interview."

5. **Rank you.** An employer has X number of positions open and X+Y number of applicants. They need to determine where you fit into the overall applicant pool.

6. **Reach a conclusion.** Employers say that they wait to make their decision after they conclude all of their interviews and review their notes. Sometimes this is true, but often the decision is made directly after the interview. I walk away from many interviews knowing that I want to hire a candidate. Unfortunately, I walk away from more interviews knowing that I definitely do not want to hire a candidate. There is a mid-level of candidates that I withhold judgment on until I see what the candidate pool looks like.

Your goal is to make the decision easy for the interviewer to make.

THE INTERVIEWEE'S PERSPECTIVE

1. **Impress the interviewer.** The person who conducts your interview holds the key to your

future. If you make a bad impression, an
interviewer has the power to close and lock the
door. You want to impress the interviewer with
everything you do and say from the first handshake
to the closing of the door behind you on the way
out.

2. **Present your case.** You need the interviewer to be
   aware of your strengths and how they make you a
   viable candidate. When you leave the room, the
   interviewer needs to have tangible evidence that
   you are the right person for the position.

3. **Learn about the position and company.** Your
   research should give you a very clear idea what the
   position entails before you reach the interview, but
   this is your opportunity to get some in-depth
   answers.

4. **See if the people at the company mesh with your
   personality type.** Interviews are an opportunity for
   both you and the company to learn about each
   other and avoid surprises in the future. You should
   try to interview at some point in the process with
   the person you will work under. Personality types

can sometimes make or break an employment opportunity.

5. **Ask for the job.** If you do not ask, you will not get. Offers of employment are like offers of marriage. They are rarely given unless the answer is already known.

If the idea of saying, "I want the job, so give it to me," makes you break out in hives, there's an easier approach.

If you know that you want the position, just let the interviewer know it.

It's as simple as, "I find this position very appealing and, if offered, I would definitely take the opportunity."

If you are still a bit unsure but you want to make sure the interviewer knows you are still interested, say "I find this position very appealing and I am interested in moving the process forward. Where do we go from here?"

PREPARATION

The only way to be great in an interview is to do great preparation.

This is true even if you have strong social skills and feel like you can just 'wing it' through the interview.

I have sat across from many competent and confident people who suddenly freeze in an interview setting.

A simple, *tell me about yourself*, can create a nervous shudder through the applicant and suddenly the only thing they can remember is their name and where they were born. It is amazing what can happen to you in an interview.

I have seen everything you can imagine.

I have had an applicant:

- Have such sweaty palms that our handshake made a loud sucking sound. I had to wipe my hand on my suit to get it dry.

- Freeze when I asked them to tell me what accomplishment gave them the greatest amount of personal pride. His eventual answer: "I can't think of anything I'm proud of."

- Start to cry because she became tongue-tied on an answer.

- Sneeze all over me by accident.

- Bleed through an entire interview because of a shaving accident in the restroom right before the interview.

- Excuse himself to the bathroom in the middle of the interview because 'I just can't hold it.'

- Have a piece of salad in her front teeth for the entire interview.

- Have such dry mouth that every word created a sticky *click* sound. There was water on the table, but he was too nervous to take a drink.

- Give me a resume with his name spelled incorrectly.

- Stare to the side or at the wall behind me for the entire interview because he was too nervous to make eye contact.

Keep in mind that I am a benevolent interviewer. I do whatever I can to make candidates feel comfortable and help to get rid of the 'jitters' as fast as possible. These types of interview missteps happen even more frequently in 'trial by fire' interviews when the interviewer actually tries to shake you up.

You only have one chance to make a good first impression. Take your preparation seriously, regardless of how confident you are in your abilities.

Trust me, you do not what to become a recruiter's funny story that they tell at the office the next day. If you are not prepared, you will be noticed, but for all the wrong reasons.

CANDIDATE, KNOW THYSELF

You are going into the interview to sell yourself, so be clear about what you have to offer.

It seems pretty simple. I mean, you are talking about a subject you know pretty well...you.

Still, it is very easy to get tongue-tied when you are trying to make a pivotal point about yourself.

Suddenly, in the middle of the interview, you become the town idiot and your answers sound like the same ones you gave in a third grade essay contest.

As soon as you leave the room, you become the most eloquent orator the world has ever seen as you think of all the great things you *could* have said.

The following exercise can save you some of this second-guessing.

Take out the paper and pen and answer these questions. Write for at least five minutes on each subject.

If you finish early, work hard to keep writing. This is usually when the good stuff comes out.

Personal Profile Worksheet

1. My five greatest strengths/character traits are:

    A. _____

    B. _____

    C. _____

    D. _____

    E. _____

2. Actions and past behavior that tangibly demonstrate these strengths are:
   (One or more detailed description for each strength.)

   A.

   B.

   C.

   D.

   E.

3. My five greatest weaknesses are:

A. _____

B. _____

C. _____

D. _____

E. _____

4. Actions that demonstrate how I overcome each of these weaknesses are:

A.

B.

C.

D.

E.

5. My three greatest accomplishments are:

   A. _____

   B. _____

   C. _____

6. I am proud of these accomplishments because:

   A.

   B.

C.

7. The greatest challenge I have had to overcome has been:

8. I am motivated by _____ because:

THE ESSENTIAL YOU EXERCISE

Now take each of the answers and re-write them as concise answers to an interview question.

Read them out loud to make sure they do not sound forced or obnoxiously formal.

Keep them under two minutes so that you do not make a series of speeches, but engage in a conversation.

When you have it nailed, memorize the answers word for word.

This will give you a solid framework to work from when you answer any question that an interviewer can throw at you. No matter what the question is, it always comes back to a few core issues.

- Who are you?

- What have you done that is impressive?

- What is it about you that will make you excel?

You have the answers in your head, but you need them at your fingertips when you are in a pressure situation.

The Essential You answers ensure the best version of you is presented in the interview and nothing gets left on the table.

WHAT TO BRING

Be prepared for every possibility.

- A good-looking brief case or attaché. If you do not have one, go pick up a synthetic leather case from Target for twenty bucks.

- Copies of your resume and cover letter in a professional looking binder.

- Typewritten questions.

- Notepad and pens.

- Your Daytimer or organizer (if you set up another interview on the spot.)

- The Essential You answers. Review them right before the interview.

- Extra everything. Be paranoid and assume you will spill coffee on yourself ten minutes before your interview, or that you will forget to brush your teeth after your pastrami sandwich at lunch. Fight back against Murphy's Law.

WHAT TO WEAR

It amazes me that there are entire books written about this one subject. It really doesn't need to be that complicated.

However, what you wear <u>does</u> matter, so it is important to understand the rules of the game.

You may not like the rules and some of them may really offend you, but fight them after you get the job. Here they are:

1. **No statements, please.** I know that you are dying to wear that cartoon tie to your first interview. Don't. You will have many opportunities in your life to demonstrate your free-spirited ways, just resist the temptation to do so in an interview. Regardless of the statement you mean to make, unconventional dress signals to a recruiter that you do not take the interview seriously. It is an insult to the recruiter who has made a time investment to interview you. This goes for all shock-value clothing and accessories.

2. **Conservative is the word.** For most professional positions, dark suit, white shirt, and conservative tie for men. Suit with a skirt for women. (Pants are considered too informal with some

recruiters.) Both sexes should pull long hair back neatly and remove any unconventional piercings. Wear minimal jewelry and make-up.

3. **Dress for your destination job.** Look better than you will ever need to for your job. Your goals are set high and you are going places. Dress like it.

Again, you might not like the rules, but there they are. While these rules apply to most interviews, be ready to adapt your dress to the industry you want to pursue.

If you interview on a construction job-site, a suit may be out of place.

If you apply to a record label to manage a punk-rock group, you might want to go *get* some body piercings.

A good rule is when in doubt, ask. If you are still in doubt, assume the most conservative.

TOP TEN RULES FOR INTERVIEW BRILLIANCE

1. **Confirm and be on time.** Being habitually late and being unemployed are closely linked. Always arrive fifteen minutes early for your appointment. If you have a long drive, assume you will have a flat tire, run out of gas, and

get lost. Plan accordingly. Call the day before the interview to confirm.

2. **Prepare and have an agenda.** You can never be too prepared. Use your parents or roommates to conduct mock interviews so you can practice the questions. Define your personal objectives before you walk into the interview. Is it to decide if you want to enter the industry? Is it to get the job? Is it to find out information specific to that particular company?

3. **First impressions are everything.** Dress like you own the place. Stand up as soon as you see the interviewer, walk toward him/her and offer your hand. Recruiters love it when candidates initiate a handshake. Make immediate eye contact and introduce yourself with confidence using your first and last name.

4. **Watch the eyes and display the teeth**. Strong eye contact is absolutely essential. If you know or have been told that this is a weakness for you, then you need to work on it. Smile pleasantly through the interview. You don't need to grin like a fool, but be pleasant and warm. This is also the best ammunition if you get stuck on a tough question. Just smile broadly and start over.

5. **Be concise.** Completely answer the questions put to you, but be concise. Try to limit your answers to a maximum of three minutes. If you are not sure if you have answered a question completely ask, "Does that answer your question, or would you like me to elaborate."

6. **Showcase The Essential You**. The biggest complaint that recruiters have is that applicants are too general. Use concrete examples to back up any claim that you make about yourself. If you say you have strong leadership skills, back it up with a brief description of your leadership experience. Use the exercises in this book to help you.

7. **Be genuine.** Don't tell your interviewer what you think they want to hear. Say what you believe. Remember that recruiters earn their living by reading people in interviews and they will see right through you if you try to be someone you are not. Be yourself.

8. **Ask intelligent questions that show you spent time preparing for the interview.** Have your list ready and make every one count.

9. **Ask for the job.** Even if you don't know if you want it. Get the job first and then make your decision. Remember the closing question, "I want to move forward. Where do we go from here?"

10. **Thank you, Thank you, Thank you.** Always send a personal thank you to your interviewer the same day you interviewed. Its arrival will be noted and its absence will be noticed.

A QUICK LITTLE INTERVIEW STORY

The hardest interview I have had in my experience was when I was going through the nomination process for Boys State when I was seventeen years old.

Boys State is a week-long program where high school boys learn about politics by actually running a political system with elections, campaigns, a visit to the state capital, and so on. It is run by the American Legion, an organization comprised of veterans of foreign wars. There were seven candidates and two spots.

I knew about the interview weeks ahead of time and I knew the format. It was going to be a panel interview with ten American Legion members and the questions were designed to see how fast you could think on your feet.

Word was that these guys liked to see the candidates squirm so they always had tough questions and liked to grill people with follow-up. I really wanted to go the Boy's State, but I was scared to death.

The big day came and I showed up a half-hour early wearing one of my Dad's ties and a suit that didn't fit quite right. The interviews were done individually in a private room off to the side from the main hall. While one of the candidates was in there getting grilled, the rest of us just milled around, joking around about the questions we were going to get. The door opened and out walked one of the candidates, a kid I knew from the high school across town.

One of the Legionnaires filled the doorway behind him and called out, "Gunhus, Jeffrey."

The Legionnaires always talked like that, very military, very intimidating.

As I walked to the door, I noticed that the kid from across town didn't look so good. He looked pretty shaken up and kind of pasty. And his hands were shaking.

Just the confidence boost I needed before I faced the firing squad.

I walked in the room and there was a single chair in the middle of the room facing a long table of the prosecutors/interviewers. Each of the Legionnaires wore their Legion hat that showed the outfit that they fought with during their respective wars, dating back to WWII.

It was an impressive show of force, clearly not designed to put a candidate at ease. The interview began.

The questions were pretty simple at first. What were my interests after school? Why did I want to go to Boy's State? Who were the public figures I admired?

Piece of cake.

Not only was I acing the thing, but I was actually enjoying it. Then one of them pulled out the heavy artillery.

"Mr. Gunhus. Do you feel that an American citizen ought to have the right to burn the American flag?"

Remember the audience. I was just asked by a room full of American Legion members, men who fought under the flag they were talking about, whether I support a person's right to burn and desecrate our national symbol.

Kind of a touchy question.

I happen to believe that burning the American flag is protected under the First Amendment and so should be allowed. For some reason, I figured that the men in room with me didn't want to hear that answer.

"Mr. Gunhus, do you have an answer to the question?"

Let me tell you, I *really* wanted to go to Boy's State. My friends and family knew I was nominated and were pulling for me, but it just seemed unlikely that my stance on flag-burning was going to help my cause. The silence stretched out a little longer, so I figured I had to say something.

"I believe that the burning of the American flag is a treacherous and shameful act."

The smiles started to appear around the table.

"An act that I could never condone nor take part in."

More smiles.

"And an act that I feel is completely protected by the First Amendment."

No more smiles.

"I feel that the flag is a symbol of the ideals of freedom and liberty, ideals that founded our country and for which we fought wars. Freedom and liberty require us to protect even those things that we disagree with, because unless we do, we are not truly free."

Good-bye Boy's State.

There was a good full minute of silence in the room (give or take fifty seconds.) Then I was excused without any further questions.

Two weeks later I was notified that I was chosen to go to Boy's State.

The notification letter had a handwritten message on the bottom from one of the Legionnaires, "Leadership is doing what you believe is right even when you believe it will be unpopular. Good luck in your future. Stay the course."

The moral of the story: being genuine is the most important thing to remember while you interview. Say what you believe and refuse to compromise yourself for any opportunity. Integrity cannot be recovered after you violate it and no job is worth that price.

HOW TO HAVE UNCOMMONLY GOOD ANSWERS TO COMMON QUESTIONS

If you want to blow away an employer, practice for an interview the same way you would prepare for an important college final.

If you were given test questions ahead of time, you would probably research the answers and make sure that you studied the right information.

You might even write out practice answers to get ready.

Well, this is a pretty important exam, so it makes sense to follow the same strategy.

Work with the most common questions asked by employers and spend some serious time deciding how you want to answer them.

Do not, I repeat, do not use this exercise to guess what the recruiter wants to hear so you can lie about your qualifications or skills.

That is not the purpose.

Your goal should be to accurately represent yourself, but to do so in a well-thought out and intelligent way.

As the saying goes, you only have one chance to make a good first impression.

Why risk a tongue-tied disaster that doesn't reflect your ability?

With a little effort, you can prepare yourself to be polished and articulate, a masterpiece of interview charm and finesse.

COMMON INTERVIEW QUESTIONS

Personal questions
1. Tell me about yourself.
2. Why are you interested in this field?
3. Why did you choose your major?
4. Why did you choose to attend your University?

5. Do you feel you received a good education? Why, why not?
6. What activities meant the most to you during college?
7. What was your favorite class in your major? Why?
8. What was your least favorite? Why?
9. What was your favorite elective class? Why?
10. What was your least favorite? Why?
11. What do you do to relax?
12. Describe a stressful situation that you have excelled in.
13. What are you most proud of in your life? Why?
14. What skills would you bring to this position?
15. Why do you think you would be an asset to our company?
16. What do you know about our industry?
17. If you couldn't be in this industry, what career would you choose?
18. What would you personally or professionally do differently?

QUESTIONS YOU NEED TO BE READY TO NAIL

1. What are your strengths and weaknesses?
2. Why are you the best person for this position?
3. Why will you be successful?
4. What motivates you?
5. Where do you want to be in five years? Ten years?
6. What is the single most important thing I should know about you?

WHEN IT'S YOUR TURN TO ASK THE QUESTIONS

The interviewer will give you the opportunity to ask your own questions at some point in the interview.

Just so you know, *I don't have any questions,* is the wrong answer.

This is a very important part of the interview because you will be evaluated by the questions you ask. A good interviewer will analyze the content of your questions, your choice of words, your delivery, and your body language. Prepare questions in advance and memorize them.

Guidelines:

1. **Make your questions reflect your ambition.** Ask about the career path for someone in your position. Make it clear that your intention is to grow quickly. Ask about what opportunities exist for professional growth such as company sponsored classes or mentor programs.

2. **Ask about your interviewer's personal experience.** You are in front of a living, breathing member of the company you are trying to join. Find out why they applied to this

company and if their expectations were met. Don't suck up. Just ask the questions that are interesting to you.

3. **Do not ask about money or benefits.** It is inappropriate in a first interview. Get the job offer first and then worry about that. If it is not what you expect, then do not accept the job. If the employer inquires why you have not asked about it, reply that you are more interested in the opportunity than the money at this point.

4. **Ask easy questions.** Do not put the interviewer on the spot with a tough question that you doubt he/she can answer. Archaic, little known bits of trivia dredged up by your research are not great opportunities to make you look smarter than your interviewer. No one likes to look foolish and it will create a negative impression in their mind.

5. **Bring written questions with you.** Place them in front of you at the beginning of the interview. Type them and write them out in complete sentences. Some recruiters ask to keep them. Do not read directly off your list. Use it as a point of reference and then ask the question with good eye contact.

6. **Take notes.** Write down key words from the answer. Don't write every word down because you lose eye contact. Also, don't try to write without looking down at all. I once had

an applicant who wrote entire paragraphs when I spoke without ever looking down. All the lines ran together and it was a complete mess. It was funny, but distracting.

7. **Never interrupt.** Let the interviewer go on as long as they want. Do not interrupt and never finish a sentence for him/her. While it's only bad manners in a regular conversation, it can be disastrous in an interview.

8. **Keep your questions short.** Restrain yourself. Remember that it is a question not an essay.

9. **Ask the closing question.** "I would like to pursue this position. Where do we go from here?"

THE SECRET TO EXCEPTIONAL ANSWERS

This is where the power of ***significant prior experience*** really comes into play.

Keep in mind that an interview is not a conversation.

A conversation is simply conveying information, while an interview is an exercise in persuasion. If you answer questions in a conversational style, all you are doing is giving an oral version of your resume.

Answers in an interview have to go beyond providing information.

Your answers have to make an argument for your aptitude and convince the interviewer that you are the right person for the position.

Every part of the interview creates the overall impression (your confidence, the way you dress, your handshake), but the content of your answers is the most important.

The formula for answering questions was actually taught to me by a candidate I interviewed.

> I asked, "Suppose you find yourself overwhelmed by the stress in your job, what would you do?"

> She replied, "Let me give you two examples of when that happened to me in past positions and how I resolved the problem…. Finally, I feel this has prepared me for this position because…"

> I asked, "Suppose you had a problem with a co-worker, how would you resolve it?"

She replied, "This happened when I was with so-and-so company and here is what I did…..However, looking at it now, I think I would have resolved it in this fashion…."

She was a great interview…and she still works for my company!

Use your *significant prior experience* to answer questions in a way that makes it impossible for an interviewer to deny you could do the job.

Most candidates will either answer my hypothetical with a hypothetical of their own.

"If that happened to me, I would do X."

Even if I like their answer, I don't feel any closer to knowing if they are right of the job or not.

Candidates with *significant prior experience* often answer these questions fairly well, but they make me work to form a conclusion.

I have to decide what character traits the experience shows and how it relates to the position I want to fill.

I have to do this mental exercise on the fly, as the question is being answered, because I have to ask another question once the answer is done.

This need to do a snap analysis can make an interviewer miss a key point and make a poor judgment about a candidate.

Help the interviewer to reach conclusions by showing him the link between your past experience and how it relates to your future position.

A simple pattern to follow is:

1. Give examples of past experience relevant to question.

2. Discuss character traits proven by experience.

3. Summarize the relevance to the position.

The questions I asked in the conversation above followed the traditional interview format. They revolved around what she could offer the company in the future and how she intended to add value through her efforts.

The candidate's answers were a persuasive argument about the character traits she developed from her past experience and why these proved that she was a good candidate for the position.

"Here are the character traits that make me a great candidate. I understand everyone says they have the same traits, but here is my proof."

Recruiters have found that the past is the best indicator of the future.

That is why relevant work experience is so welcome. If you have performed well in the past, there is no reason to think you will not continue to do so.

On the same logic, if you were a real slacker the last time you had significant responsibilities, there is not much reason to doubt that you will be a slacker again.

This may seem like a very narrow way of thinking, but it makes good business sense.

Hiring people is like approving a credit card. The first thing a bank does when they receive your credit application is review your past credit and payment history. The person reviewing your credit does not want to read an essay on all the reasons why you are a trustworthy investment for the bank to make. All the bank wants to know is, "Have you paid your obligations in the past?" If you have not, they will not be willing to take a risk on you.

I do believe people can change.

The past is not a prison that traps you to a predetermined fate and every individual has the power of personal change.

Just like the person who goes bankrupt and then rebuilds their credit over a period of time, a person who makes bad choices early in their life can rebuild their credibility over time.

However, when I hire someone, I want to know they can do the job right now.

Traditional interviews test how well you can think and imagine solutions to future problems. In a world of low unemployment and companies competing for graduating seniors, this was as good as it often got for interviewers. Candidates didn't have much experience but you had to hire someone for the position you were trying to fill.

Now that there is more competition for jobs, interviewers can hold out for candidates with more previous experience and conduct a behavioral interview. This type of interview tries to determine behavior patterns as demonstrated by the problems or situations you have dealt with in the past.

Not only that, but in today's job market, I have my pick of many qualified candidates.

Why would I choose someone without _significant prior experience_ and the ability to talk about it skillfully?

To be successful in a behavioral interview you need to demonstrate a link between your past actions and actions you will need to take in your new job.

If you really want to be ready to ace any interview, complete the exercise below to identify the evidence that you are going to use to make this link.

Warning: You just might find out from this exercise that you do not have enough proof of your talent and character yet. If this is the case (and it often is if you're honest with yourself), review the chapter on developing your experience base through internships.

Like anything else, the easiest option is to skip out and not do the work in this section. I'm as guilty as the next guy in skipping exercises when I'm reading a book.

However, if you are serious about making a difference in your career search outcome, we need to dig in and get to work.

So, go find a pen, turn off the cell phone, and commit the half hour to really do this correctly. You won't regret it.

<u>Behavior Worksheet</u>

Directions: List two specific stories that demonstrate positive behavior in each of these areas. Use the most recent examples first.

1. You demonstrated leadership in past roles.

   a.

   b.

2. You demonstrated work ethic by doing whatever it takes to complete a job.

   a.

   b.

3. You demonstrated perseverance by overcoming repeated failure to finally succeed at your goals.

   a.

   b.

4. You resolved a conflict with a supervisor or a co-worker in a professional manner.

   a.

   b.

5. You demonstrated initiative by creating a new project or solving a problem that was not your responsibility.

   a.

   b.

6. You handled stress and achieved your goals.

    a.

    b.

7. You demonstrated creativity in your problem-solving.

    a.

    b.

8. You demonstrated your ambition by the determination of your actions.

    a.

    b.

It is important for you to take the time to fill out this exercise. Draw from as many different experiences as possible.

Behavior that you demonstrate in a non-work setting is just as valid as what you do on the job.

The interviewer wants to know what kind of person you are, not necessarily what kind of worker bee you have been in the past.

I spend a lot of time in my interviews talking about leadership. I can't tell you the number of times candidates have told me that they really don't have any leadership experience.

I always probe to see if they have done any sports, clubs, etc. Suddenly, the floodgates are open. "I was the Varsity football captain." "I was the founder of the Business Club on campus."

Everything you do has a bearing on the kind of person you are and the behavior traits that you will demonstrate in your career.

Go back in time and show a pattern of behavior that demonstrates positive character traits. It can be something that happened in your family, while you were playing sports, or in a past job.

A QUICK STORY

I once interviewed a candidate with extremely limited work experience and marginal interpersonal skills. Ten minutes into the interview I made a decision not to hire this person.

My last question was whether he could describe to me a circumstance where he had to show incredible determination and perseverance in order to reach a goal.

Honestly, I didn't expect a great answer, but I received one that I will never forget.

This young man had been nearly beaten to death by his father when he was three years old and raised in poverty by his single mother. He was surrounded by gangs, drugs, and crime throughout his adolescence and became involved in all three. After barely passing High School, a strong male role model convinced him to attend junior college to further his education. He did so and married his pregnant high school sweetheart that same year.

Determined to set a good example for his newborn, he maintained a 4.0 average throughout his first year in college and transferred to a four-year university. After he transferred, his daughter was diagnosed with a rare brain disorder that required several surgeries. The prognosis gave his daughter a 10% chance to live past her third birthday. To help pay the medical bills not covered by his insurance, this person worked nights at UPS, attended school during the day, and still wanted to do my program so he could show his daughter that hard work creates success.

This was the person I was about to turn away because I didn't think he possessed the determination and the will power to be in my program. He went on to be a valuable employee and it taught me a lesson about judging too quickly.

If you can give a recruiter a concrete image of positive character traits, you have won half the battle.

Skills can be taught, but character traits are incredibly hard to instill in someone. Demonstrate through exact, detailed examples that you have the skills and behavior patterns that you claim to possess.

Do not leave a recruiter guessing whether they can believe that you can handle the job, make your case through the evidence of your past actions.

INTERVIEW SECRETS THAT PREFESSIONAL RECRUITERS DON'T WANT YOU TO KNOW

SECRET #1

Some recruiters do not interview well. You will find that everyone you interview with will have an individual style. Some recruiters will provide you with great opportunities to showcase your talents and past experiences.

Some recruiters will give you a half-hour lecture on the importance of your work ethic and a not-so-brief history of their own lives.

A bad interviewer can be dangerous to you.

They still represent your link to the company or the position that you want and their lack of ability could seriously impact your ability to showcase your attributes. Do not allow poor interview skills to sabotage your chances.

Take responsibility in the interview to get your most important points across.

If the interviewer does not ask very good questions, use your questions as a stepping stone to the answers you want to give.

"How important do you feel leadership skills are to this position?"

"Great, because I have consistently shown leadership ability throughout my college career. For example, ..."

Do not let an interviewer take away from your ability to get your main points across.

If you are frustrated throughout the interview, give a strong closing argument at the end.

"In closing, I would like to reiterate why I would be a good investment for you and for the company. Every hiring decision you make is an investment decision. And like any investment decision, I'm sure you base your decision on risk. Although I am confident that I would be a good choice for you to make, I understand it is my responsibility to convince you why I am a good risk.

First, the best indicator of future action is past results. I have been a consistent high-performer in any activity where I have applied myself. For example....

Second, the most important precursor to achievement is commitment. I am committed to my career goals and I believe that ABC Corp is the best vehicle for me to realize my ambitions. I would be asset if hired for this position.

I am very interested in this position. How can I move forward from this point?"

SECRET #2

Mirror the person who interviews you.
This is an old sales technique. The theory is that people respond to people that are like themselves.

A hard-hitting, down-to-business-type will not like to work with someone who is easy-going and soft-spoken.

Likewise, a quiet, diminutive personality will go into shock when confronted with someone who is brash and overbearing.

When you enter an interview, determine the personality traits of the interviewer and mirror what you see.

If you get a rapid talking showman, you had better step up the energy level.

If you get a mouse, don't feel like you have to stoop all the way to their level, but you might want to tone down your delivery a little.

People like to hire people that are like themselves.

The more similarity you can make the interviewer see in you the better. The old joke about interviewer egos: *How was the interview?* That guy was perfect. He was just like me! You may laugh, but often this is the way it works.

SECRET #3

Recruiters are bored to death. Try having the same conversation twenty times in a row and you will have a flavor of what it means to be a full time recruiter.

If you can break the monotony, you will stand out.

Do whatever it takes to be interesting. Dare to be bold and outgoing, but don't overdo it. Find one thing you have in common with the interviewer and use that to have a brief non-work oriented conversation. Show how friendly and easy to get along with you will be once you're hired.

SECRET #4

Recruiters have egos. Yes, it's true. Recruiters, like most people, like to talk about how great they are. Don't shamelessly pander to their ego, but show an interest in their careers and background. Be careful, because some people need very little prompting to open the floodgates and you are not there to find out the interviewer's life story. Ask enough to make them feel good and to get some insight into what their experience with the company has been.

SECRET #5

Recruiters will forget everything you say. The exact words that you use in the interview are going to be forgotten. The only thing a recruiter will remember is an overall impression.

The words you use are important, because they create the impression, but your mannerisms are just as important.

When I review my notes the day after a full interview schedule, I remember the candidates based on their aptitude and their overall presentation.

Were they confident?

Quiet?

Were they forceful with their answers?

Was it an enjoyable conversation, or were they difficult to talk to?

Mannerisms count, so be aware of how you carry yourself.

Your words and answers will prove your aptitude, but employers look at attitude just as strongly.

Say the right things, and remember to say them well.

THE LAST WORD

- Don't confuse an interview with a snapshot of the true you. An interview is you on your best professional behavior with the advantage of intense preparation and extensive research.

- Preparation for an interview includes knowing specific background about the company with which you are interviewing and being able to clearly articulate your skills, interests, and goals.

- You are judged by the quality of your questions as much as the quality of your answers.

- The key to excellent interview answers is to use specific examples from your past that demonstrate the claims you make about the character traits you possess.

CHAPTER SIX

TOP-DOWN JOB HUNTING

The Secret Method To Get Any Job You Want

I was fortunate that my first job out of college was to take over and run a million dollar business that I had been involved with since I was 18 (and still run today).

However, before I made the decision to take the path I did, I aggressively sought out career opportunities using the methods I'm about to describe.

The results were fantastic.

I considered the entertainment industry and ended up with an hour long meeting with a VP for ICM, one of the top talent agencies in the world.

I thought commodities trading would be of interest, so I spent an afternoon with one of the leading traders for Merrill Lynch and a day with a series of owners of brokerage houses in Chicago.

Politics has always been exciting to me, so I spent a day with a Congressional candidate and a renowned national political strategist.

All of these meetings led to job offers.

I declined all of them...but it was nice to be asked.

FIRST, A WARNING

Teaching you this method is not without its risks. It kind of like giving you a loaded gun, leaving you alone on a target range and saying,

"Just hold on to that and I'll come back in a few months when you're good and ready and teach you how to shoot that thing."

As soon as I walk around the corner, the gun's going to go off. The temptation to try it out would just be too much to bear.

And that's how people get hurt.

There's a real good chance you are not ready to use the method I'm about to teach you.

The problem with that if you go ahead and try to use it anyway, is that you're going to blow it. And when you blow it, you really blow it because you can go to this well exactly one time.

There is only one bullet in the gun…so don't fire until you're sure you're ready.

Go back and review the section on creating marketable skills in yourself and building your resume with ***significant prior experience***.

You must already be an irresistible candidate before you attempt Top-Down Job Hunting.

The old saying is true. You have but one chance to make a first impression.

Don't blow yours.

THE TRADITIONAL JOB SEARCH IS DEAD

Traditional methods all point you toward human resource departments and professional recruiters.

While you will receive job offers using traditional entry points, approximately 70% of jobs are filled outside of these avenues.

A majority of positions are filled through referrals, networking, and personal relationships. Therefore, if you confine yourself to traditional job searching techniques, you are severely limiting your options.

So, if this hidden job market is filled through connections, how do you magically get the connections to help your career?

Instead of starting at the bottom of the interview food chain with the Assistant-Recruiter-In-Training, I am going to show you how to start at the top and work your way down.

You may not have the connections right now to enter the hidden job market, but if you work hard using the methods in this chapter, you will have connections that will help you throughout your career.

THE PREMISE

- The only time you want to visit Human Resources or Personnel Department is after you have been hired or after you have a ringing endorsement from a senior executive.

- The more people you meet in your industry, the more opportunity you have of job offers.

- The most powerful people in your industry will be able to open the most doors for you.

- People love to help college students and will give you incredible access to try to help you.

- Access is only the beginning. You still have to shine once you get there.

DEFINE YOUR TARGETS

Identify the industry you want to target. Hopefully, this is relatively easy for you and you have a destination job in mind. If you find yourself in the middle of your Pre-Life Crisis and can't seem to figure out what you want to do with your future, check out my book Choose The Right Career. In it, you will find a series of exercises designed to show you how to choose the perfect career path based on your interests, skills and passions. If you already know what you want to do, you're ready to move on to the next step.

Research the industry and find out the names of principals. Create a target list of the heavy hitters in your industry. Start off with the easy ones. The big names.

If you want to go into the film/entertainment field start your list with Brian Grazer, Steven Spielberg, and Robert Zemeckis. If you want to go into investment banking, find out who the current heads are of the top investment banking firms in the industry. Make the list as extensive and as extravagant as you want.

Identify some of the mid-level players in the industry. This can be a little more difficult because the celebrity factor is gone. A good source of information is the annual reports for public companies. Another good source is a publication called the Who's Who In American Business. This book is categorized by industry, which makes it a very useful tool for your purpose.

The people to locate are the mid-level movers and shakers. These are the people who are playing the game and playing it well. They have rocketed through the ranks, experienced early success, and are eager to tell someone about it.

If you are interested in advertising, find a young ad executive who recently received a big promotion. If you are interested in sales, find someone who has recently won an award or set a company record. You can find this information in your local newspaper's business section. There is usually a column with a title like "Executive's On The Move," "Movers and Shakers," or something similar.

SEND A GREAT LETTER

Now that you have identified your targets, it's time to write a great letter. The letter serves only one purpose, to open the person up to the possibility of some type of interaction with you. Whether it is a phone call, a personal meeting, or a message left with a secretary, all you want is contact.

SAMPLE TOP-DOWN LETTER

Dear Mr. Spielberg,

My name is Spencer Pepe and I am writing to ask for a ten minute meeting with you to discuss the film industry.

I will graduate from the University of California at Santa Barbara later this year and I am considering a career in film production. However, I have several concerns about what that career would be like. I write to you because the impact of your work is one of the reasons I feel compelled toward a film career.

I understand that your time is incredibly valuable. However, I was hoping that you could find ten minutes to meet with me to answer a few questions. I will call your office at 9 am on Monday, September 13, to ask your assistant if there would be a convenient time for us to meet.

Sincerely,

Spencer Pepe

P.S. If your schedule does not permit a meeting, can you suggest someone I could contact to answer my questions?

The key is to make it clear that you are not looking for a job, but simply want to discuss the concerns you have about a career in the field.

"Concern" is the key word. Remember that the letter is written to an industry leader, someone who loves what they do. They are eager to make others understand why they love their field. The thought of someone with concerns about such a great career is almost too much to bear.

Be completely honest in your letters and be respectful.

Do not tell some mid-level ad executive that she is the reason you want to go into advertising.

But you can say, "I saw the announcement of your promotion in the Wall Street Journal. Congratulations! I recently graduated from the University of Florida and I am considering a career in advertising and I found it encouraging to read about your success....."

The P.S. at the bottom is essential.

The Top Down Method assumes that the big-time players will shoot you down (and typically never sees the letter). Sometimes you get some amazing luck and you will actually get the ten minutes you request.

Usually the best you can hope for is an answer to your last question, 'Whom else can I contact?'

If you get an answer to this question, you are doing great.

If Steven Spielberg refers you to someone, there are a few things you need to understand.

First, accept the fact that Steven Spielberg did not see your letter, but that it was answered by an assistant.

Second, realize that you shouldn't care because all that matters now is that you can write a letter to your new contact that says,

"Dear Mr. Smith, Steven Spielberg's office suggested that I contact you."

How powerful is that?

Make sure that you immediately send Steven Spielberg and his staff thank-you cards and some flowers for the help. Include a note with the flowers that explains what they are for and that you intend to contact Mr. So-and-so.

Again, Steven Spielburg never sees the flowers, but you have reminded his office staff who you are. If Mr. Smith calls to ask who you are, you now have a chance that someone in the office will say something good about you.

I know it sounds like a lot of work, but the contacts you can make with this method can be incredible.

BE SHARP ON THE PHONE

In your letter, you need to give a definite date and time that you will call your contact. This makes it harder to chicken out and decide not to call. Make sure that you call on time and are prepared to be sharp.

If you are calling a mid-level player, there is a fifty-fifty chance you will speak with someone who expects your call, whether it is your target person or a personal assistant.

10 - 15% of the time, you will make the phone call and be put directly through to the person you want to reach.

When you call a big shot, there is a 1% chance you will talk to the person, but there is always the possibility, so be ready.

You have to make this a <u>great</u> phone call.

Write an outline for the phone call before you make it. Double-check your contact information and clearly define the purpose for your call.

Have your schedule ready so that you can set an appointment. If it is a heavy-hitter, cancel everything on your schedule if they agree to a meeting.

Be prepared to conduct your ten-minute interview over the phone if that is all the person can offer you.

There is nothing more embarrassing than going through all this trouble and then not having a single question to ask.

Remember that your goal is to get a personal meeting, so make certain that you ask for one.

Be considerate of the person's time. Try to set up an interview time early in the conversation and then let them go back to work.

If you can only reach an assistant, explain your situation and inquire whether your contact received your letter.

Assistants rule the world, so take the time to gain their approval.

They can be a great allies. If you can win over the personal assistant, your letter might reach the contact's desk instead of the trash-can. It's amazing what a little kindness can accomplish!

THE MEETING: ONLY THE BRILLIANT NEED ATTEND

Treat this meeting as you would any interview. The difference is that you are the one who gets to conduct the questioning.

This may be very uncommon ground for you, which is a great reason to do a lot of preparation.

- **Ask great questions:** You are not there to apply for a job, so don't feel like you need to throw softballs. Ask about the drawbacks of the industry, find out what the trade-offs for success are, and find the steps you need to take to achieve prominence in the industry.

Write down twice as many questions as you think you will have time to ask. You will be surprised how fast you go through them.

10 GREAT QUESTIONS

1. Why did you go into this field?
2. What has been the biggest challenge in your career?
3. How has the industry changed since you started?
4. How do you see the industry evolving in the next five years?

5. What path would you recommend to enter this career field successfully?
6. What skills and character traits are essential to be successful in this industry?
7. Are there negatives to this industry? What are they?
8. What is your reading list like? What books would you recommend?
9. If you were me, an over-eager, confident, impatient, recent college graduate, what would you do to make certain that you were successful?
10. What businesses and individuals do you respect the most in this industry? Why?

8 QUESTIONS NOT TO ASK

1. How can I get your job? *Cliché*
2. How can you help me? *Clumsy*
3. How much money can I make? *Immature*
4. How much free time will I have? *Lazy*
5. Why would I want to be in this industry? *Arrogant*
6. What can you tell me about your job? *Non-specific*
7. What mistakes have you made that held you back in your career? *Awkward*
8. Do you feel like you had to be unethical to be successful? *Judgmental*

- **State your purpose and do not bring a resume:** Re-enforce the point you made in your letter that you want to consider a future in the field and only requested the meeting to find out more about what such a career would entail. If they ask for a resume, say "I didn't bring a resume with me because I am truly here only to find out more about this career. I would love to give you a copy later to get your insight and suggestions."

- **Share information about yourself.** The person you are meeting with will inevitably ask you questions about yourself. Be open, but do not use your regular interview style. Be much more conversational so that the meeting does not turn into an interview.

- **Ask the best question.** "If you were me, and you wanted to excel in this industry, what would you do?" There is wisdom to be learned in the answer to this question. The contact will often offer assistance to you at this point if you have made a good impression. As in, "If I were you, I would get into the trainee program at corporate headquarters. I can't get you the job, but I can make sure that the right people see your resume." Bingo.

- **Be considerate of the person's time.** This is where I always mess up. I lined up a ten-minute meeting with the Vice-President of ICM, a Hollywood talent agency with a client list including Schwarzenegger and the Beach Boys. I asked that man questions for an hour and a half! Granted, he never asked me to leave, but the signs were there that the interview had dragged on too long. Don't cut an interview short if you are rolling, but respect people's time. They will appreciate it and be happy to help you in the future.

- **Ask for help.** Sometimes people are willing to help you, but they need a little encouragement. If you have established a good rapport with the contact, ask them who else they could refer you to in the industry to get some more insight. If you do not feel comfortable, simply ask if you can contact them in the future if you think of any more questions. Just make sure that the door is left open for you.

FOLLOWING UP/SUCKING UP...SAME THING

You worked hard to make this contact, so don't ruin all of your effort because you forgot to follow-up.

Send an immediate thank-you card. If you were able to keep the meeting focused on questions about the industry, and were able to escape from the meeting turning into a formal job interview, send a small gift as well. Some small bit of memorabilia from your school will do nicely.

<u>Never</u> do this after a regular interview as it can come across as extremely unprofessional, but it can work wonders after an informational interview.

Is this sucking up?

Of course it is! And it works great!

If the interview went well, you were probably offered some kind of assistance. Either a contact name, an offer for a job interview, or some good advice.

Follow-up as soon as possible on whatever action your contact suggested. Keep your contact informed of your progress and always ask for more advice.

To avoid being a nuisance, limit your contact to a maximum once every two weeks.

WHY IT WORKS SO WELL

1. **People are basically good. They like to help students and people about to start their careers.** People who are very successful in their fields will often teach toward the end of their careers to fulfill the need to 'give back.' Often, when a heavy hitter grants you an interview, you will find that they had a similar experience when they were your age. Bill Clinton was famous (and notorious) for spending time with the interns and students who visited the White House. His formative experience meeting John F. Kennedy when he was a student compelled him to give the same experience to others.

2. **People all have the same favorite subject of conversation, themselves.** You provide them with a forum to brag a little and to feel important. This is especially true for mid-level players who have recently received a promotion.

3. **People look out for their investments.** After you have an informational interview with someone, they tend to take an interest in your success. This is because they have invested their time and they want to see their investment pay off. Also, your contact will be eager to see if you follow the advice that they have given. They

are able to live vicariously through your experiences, and want their recommendations to be proven correct. "See, I told you that if you called So-and-so you would get a good job offer."

4. **Informational interviews are easy work.** You are not explicitly asking for anything other than some advice. The person you are interviewing does not have to make any decisions or take any actions as a result of your meeting. It usually represents a nice break from a heavy schedule.

5. **Interview rules are suspended.** While you need to be polite, well dressed, etc., you can ask much tougher questions and be much more conversational than if you were in a formal interview. The people you interview recognize this and look forward to an interesting dialogue instead of the usual rigid formality of an interview.

6. **You cannot have a bad experience.** Well, as long as you don't throw up on yourself or do anything bizarre. Outside of that, any contact with someone in your industry is educational. If you are able to meet a legend in your field, it can be a transforming experience. Go into every meeting with an open mind and be ready to

learn. After the interview, immediately write down everything you can remember from the conversation.

THE LAST WORD

- Top-Down Job Hunting is a technique designed to put you in touch directly with the decision-makers in your industry.

- Successful people enjoy talking about themselves and are usually very willing to grant you an informational interview. These often lead to job offers and can create an impressive networking list in your industry.

- Prepare for each meeting like it is the interview that will change your life. It very well could be just that.

CHAPTER SEVEN

GET LUCKY

It's hard to detect good luck – it looks so much like something you've earned.

-Fred Clark

Now that you now know how to arm yourself for battle and engage in high-end tactics to give yourself an almost unfair advantage, I want to talk to you about winning the war.

It's not enough to get your foot in the door. It's not enough for you to get the job offer.

We need to figure out how to keep you in the room and for you to get the success you want.

Success is a strange word. For as many people as there are willing to peddle you some magical method to attain it, or teach you some secret formula to possess it, you would imagine it's a tangible *thing*. You know. Something you can possess. Hold on to. Frame and put on your wall.

Well, you might be young, but you're not stupid, right?

You've already figured out that this "success" thing people keep talking about is more abstract, more an imagined and shifting thing.

Early on, probably starting in Junior High, I became interested in why some people achieved more than others.

Why some people just seemed to get more done in a single lifetime then nearly everyone else around them.

One of my hobbies became to collect information from very successful people to determine what made them a success. It's a hobby I continue to this day.

I use autobiographies, second-hand accounts, and personal interviews to try and get down to the elemental ingredients for success.

One of my favorite conversations was with my own grandfather, a retired two-star General and World War II veteran. I want to share it with you because, at its heart, it tells you everything you need to know to be successful.

My grandfather, General Joe May had a successful military career and rose through the ranks by placing first or second in every officer training class he attended.

He spent his career also trying to learn how successful men designed their lives and carried themselves. His exposure to successful individuals was broader than my own as he was able to speak with major military leaders, governors, and several U.S. Presidents.

I sat down with him as I entered my own pre-life crisis, frantically deciding what to do after graduation, and asked him for advice.

I wanted to know what made success.

What were the secrets he had learned through those years of development and exposure to major personalities?

He was quiet for a while, eyes squinting slightly as he formulated his answer.

I waited for what I knew would be life-changing advice.

"Every person I know who was truly successful..." he started, "all possessed the same fundamental quality."

Now I'm dying.

What was this one quality?

What was the secret?

"Every person who is successful is that way because they are extremely lucky."

Lucky! This is the great advice I get to steer me on my future! What a rip-off!

"But," he continued, "you have to define luck in a very specific way. Luck is when opportunity meets preparation."

Luck = Opportunity + Preparation

Now, General Joe wasn't the first to make this point. (This quote has been attributed as far back as Seneca, the Roman philosopher in mid-1st century AD.) But coming from my grandfather, I paid close attention to what it really meant.

If we look at this statement as a mathematical equation, there are two constants and one variable.

Luck, which can also be termed "the result" or "success", is a constant because we determine how it is defined. Everyone perceives success in different ways. If you get a big promotion at work, one of your friends might congratulate you, while the other feels bad for you because you will now have more responsibility and less free time. You define luck/success for yourself.

Opportunity is also a constant. I often get an argument on this point because there is privilege in the world and not all opportunity is equal.

However, I have met people from an extremely privileged background who have done nothing with their lives, and I have met people who have risen from abject poverty to accomplish amazing tasks. Is it more difficult to rise from poverty than to slide into the family business?

Absolutely.

But opportunity exists, and it can be captured. While the ease of capturing opportunity varies, the existence of those who overcame great personal odds to rise to high office or station clearly demonstrates opportunity exists for all.

That leaves only one variable, preparation.

People can personally define success, and opportunity exists for everyone, but preparation is usually where the equation breaks down.

What are you willing to do so that you can take advantage of opportunity and create the luck you want?

For example, I interview people all the time who want to go into international business. This is an exciting and high growth field with incredible opportunity. I ask them what languages they are willing to learn to be a success in this field. Nine times out of ten, the candidate says they do not like languages and are going to work with English speaking countries. Obviously, someone who is not willing to prepare for a career in international business by learning a language will not be very "lucky" when the time comes to enter the job market.

Preparation never stops because:

1. **You can always improve.** The greatest athletes always practice the most. They are the first on the field and work hard to always improve.

2. **Opportunity is unpredictable.** You never know when new options will present themselves. The key is to be prepared to take advantage of any opportunity that serves as a vehicle for your skills. Suppose you meet someone who owns their own business and they need a new director of sales and they have to hire someone right away. If you have created a strong background built on concrete results, you just got "lucky."

Pursue luck/success through preparation. If the preparation is difficult then you have to gauge the level of commitment to your goals. This comes from an internal conversation you need to have with yourself about your goals. Once you commit, though, that's it.

Don't waffle. Don't equivocate.

Don't blubber that what you're trying to accomplish is too hard, takes too long or that life is unfair.

Either commit to your goals 100% and engage in the actions necessary for their achievement...or change them.

That last comment might surprise you, but it's important to understand that it is OK to change your goals.

The trick to changing your goals is to make certain you are changing them for the right reasons.

If you are changing because your initial goals are "too hard," "require more work than I thought," "are too unrealistic," or anything in this vein, then you are selling yourself short.

If you are going to make a big change in direction, make certain it is direction only, and not reach.

What do I mean by "reach?"

The reach of your goals measures their difficulty level and whether they are truly an aggressive attempt to fulfill your potential.

Change direction if you feel you must, but do not let a course correction act as a cover for downgrading your ambition. To change direction is human. To maintain the reach of your goals is divine.

A FINAL THOUGHT

Thank you for sharing with me the few hours you spent reading this book. I hope that you took from it strategies and ideas that will impact your life in positive ways.

Please remember that anything worth doing is going to be hard. The very best things are going to be the hardest of all. Your job is to never give up on your dreams and ambitions. There is amazing power in the simple decision that your goals are non-negotiable...and that decision is yours alone to make.

We all get exactly one life to live. Make yours worthwhile and without regret. It is the greatest gift you can give to yourself. May you enjoy your personal journey and be blessed with unlimited luck of your own creation.

Additional Titles from The Career Series

HOW TO CHOOSE THE RIGHT CAREER...You So Don't Waste Your Life In A Job You Can't Stand.

ISBN 1-4486-7959-1

$16.95 (paperback)
$14.95 (ebook)

You're going to spend half your waking hours either at work or thinking about work. Isn't it worthwhile to make sure you're choosing the right career? **How To Choose The Right Career** *takes away the guesswork and shows you how to confidently make the right decision.*

With simple to use exercises and techniques, you will be able to finally figure out exactly what you want for a career. Even if you think you know what you want to do, shouldn't you make sure you're headed in the right direction before you begin the journey?

GET YOUR COPY AND ACCESS FREE CAREER ADVICE AT

www.thecareerseries.com

7242518R0

Made in the USA
Charleston, SC
08 February 2011